Devotions on the
Hebrew Bible

Devotions on the Hebrew Bible

54 REFLECTIONS TO INSPIRE & INSTRUCT

Milton Eng and Lee M. Fields, General Editors

ZONDERVAN

Devotions on the Hebrew Bible
Copyright © 2015 by Milton Eng and Lee M. Fields

Requests for information should be addressed to:
Zondervan, 3900 *Sparks Dr. SE, Grand Rapids, Michigan 49546*

Library of Congress Cataloging-in-Publication Data

    Devotions on the Hebrew Bible : 53 reflections to inspire and instruct / edited by Milton Eng and Lee M. Fields.
       pages   cm
    Includes bibliographical references and index.
    ISBN 978-0-310-49453-9 (softcover)
    1. Bible. Old Testament. Hebrew — Versions. 2. Bible. Old Testament — Meditations. I. Eng, Milton, editor.
BS718.D47   2015
242'.5 — dc23   2015020811

Cover design: Mark Novelli, www.imagocreative.com
Cover photo: The Center for the Study of New Testament Manuscripts,
        www.csntm.org
Interior design: Matthew Van Zomeren & Kait Lamphere

Printed in the United States of America

HB 09.05.2023

Table of Contents[*]

---

[*] Please note that the devotions are arranged in Hebrew canonical order. See page 11 for a chart delineating the Hebrew canonical arrangement with English translation.

Arrangement of Old Testament Books in the Hebrew Bible

LAW	
Hebrew Name	English Name
בְּרֵאשִׁית	Genesis
שְׁמוֹת	Exodus
וַיִּקְרָא	Leviticus
בְּמִדְבַּר	Numbers
דְּבָרִים	Deuteronomy

WRITINGS	
Hebrew Name	English Name
תְּהִלִּים	Psalms
אִיּוֹב	Job
מִשְׁלֵי	Song of Songs
רוּת	Ruth
שִׁיר הַשִּׁירִים	Song of Songs
קֹהֶלֶת	Ecclesiastes
אֵיכָה	Lamentations
אֶסְתֵּר	Esther
דָּנִיֵּאל	Daniel
עֶזְרָא	Ezra
נְחֶמְיָה	Nehemiah
דִּבְרֵי הַיָּמִים	1 – 2 Chronicles

PROPHETS	
Hebrew Name	English Name
יְהוֹשֻׁעַ	Joshua
שֹׁפְטִים	Judges
שְׁמוּאֵל	1 – 2 Samuel
מְלָכִים	1 – 2 Kings
יְשַׁעְיָהוּ	Isaiah
יִרְמְיָהוּ	Jeremiah
יְחֶזְקֵאל	Ezekiel
הוֹשֵׁעַ	Hosea
יוֹאֵל	Joel
עָמוֹס	Amos
עֹבַדְיָה	Obadiah
יֹנָה	Jonah
מִיכָה	Micah
נַחוּם	Nahum
חֲבַקּוּק	Habakkuk
צְפַנְיָה	Zephaniah
חַגַּי	Haggai
זְכַרְיָה	Zechariah
מַלְאָכִי	Malachi

To Verlyn D. Verbrugge,
editor, author, scholar, friend

Introduction

In 2012 Zondervan published *Devotions on the Greek New Testament.* Independently and unbeknownst to each other, Milton and Lee approached Verlyn Verbrugge about doing a companion volume for the Hebrew Old Testament. Verlyn then asked if we would co-edit such a volume. What a blessing and surprise to learn that we two old friends would be working on this project together! *Soli Deo Gloria.*

The aim of this book is twofold: (1) to encourage students and pastors to continue (or to resume!) using their Hebrew knowledge in their devotions and sermon preparation and (2) to demonstrate that a knowledge of the original languages can and should be a spiritually rewarding exercise. Consequently, each devotion is designed to bring out some grammatical or lexical insight which cannot be gained in English translation alone along with some point of spiritual application. As Lee often says in his classes, "Bible study is never complete until it results in worship."

There is both unity and diversity among the contributors. All hold a doctorate degree and are evangelical in theology. However, they also represent a diversity of backgrounds. There are men and women representing various denominations. Some live in countries outside the United States. Some are highly published, while others are not. Most are professors, but there is also a Bible translator. All have a clear call to ministry. No one has contributed more than two devotions.

The devotions are arranged in biblical order following the Hebrew arrangement — an opportunity for teaching. Thankfully, we have been able to provide a devotion for each of the thirty-nine books of the Old Testament. Of course, some books have attracted more devotions than others (i.e., Genesis, Isaiah, and Psalms) but we have covered all the genres and divisions of the Hebrew Bible.

Authors were asked to start their devotion with a standard English translation (e.g., NIV, NRSV, ESV) but were encouraged to use other translations or even their own translation thereafter. The reader will find a variety of linguistic features highlighted among these fifty-four devotions, including wordplays, word studies, and literary and grammatical analyses. References to the Septuagint and implications for the New Testament are also noted. All this in devotions of approximately 600 words and limited footnotes! We have included indices of Grammatical Terms and Hebrew Words to help Hebrew teachers find that perfect illustration for their teaching.

Milton and Lee wish to thank all the contributors who took time out of their busy schedules to write. It is especially gratifying to have former teachers, current mentors, and fellow classmates contribute to this project. In reading through their devotions, we have been deeply humbled by the faith and spirituality of our colleagues in the field. Their own enthusiasm for the project was especially encouraging. Thanks are due also to Zondervan for agreeing to produce this work and to Verlyn Verbrugge and Nancy Erickson, who guided two novices through the ins and outs of editing. Their encouragement and wise counsel made this work a joy and immeasurably better. In fact, without them, this could not have been completed.

Finally, we have indeed dedicated this volume to Verlyn. During the final stages of this project, he was diagnosed with pancreatic cancer and fell asleep in the Lord on Father's Day, June 21, 2015. We grieve deeply over the loss of his grace and Christian presence that made us feel special in a big world — just as Jesus would do. "Precious in the sight of the LORD is the death of his faithful servants." (Ps 116:15)

As we present this volume, *DHB*, our hope and prayer is that readers would be drawn to a deeper love for, understanding of, and adherence to the Scriptures and the God who gave them, and that God himself might be glorified thereby.

Milton Eng and Lee Fields,
editors and contributors

A Faith That Grows

GENESIS 15:6

MT	ESV
וְהֶאֱמִן בַּיהוָה וַיַּחְשְׁבֶהָ לּוֹ צְדָקָה׃	And he believed the LORD, and he counted it to him as righteousness.

Genesis 15:6 was an important verse for Paul (Rom 4:3; Gal 3:6) and James (2:23). There are distinctions in the Hebrew text that help us understand their different emphases.

The first word in Hebrew is וְהֶאֱמִן ("and he was believing"), not וַיַּאֲמֵן ("and he believed"), as the ESV and most English versions read. The verb וְהֶאֱמִן is an open-ended tense in Hebrew that is not used very often. Typically, in past contexts this tense is used when repetition is involved, like in Genesis 29:2–3. (This observation applies to both *weqatal* and *yiqtol*.) More rarely this tense is used to mark open-endedness, as in Genesis 2:25, וְלֹא יִתְבֹּשָׁשׁוּ, "they were not ashamed ..." [not וְלֹא הִתְבֹּשָׁשׁוּ!]. The tense is used to provocatively present an open-ended stage for the following story of Genesis 3. (See 1 Sam 1:10 "was crying," 1:12 "while it was happening," and 1:13 "was not being heard" for more examples of the open-ended use of this tense.)

The Hebrew verb וְהֶאֱמִן looks at the process of believing without looking at the beginning or end of the "believing." The tense does not imply that Abram first believed God at this point. Nor does it present Abram's faith as complete at this point. Abram had started to trust Yahweh's promises when he travelled to Canaan in Genesis 12. And the author's choice of this tense at 15:6 forces the reader to think about ongoing implications. In a real sense, Abram's faith was a lifelong "walk." His faith matured and was tested. The most climactic test comes later in Genesis 22 with the command to sacrifice Isaac. James specifically makes the link between Genesis 15 and Genesis 22. James may have been aware of the open-ended nature of וְהֶאֱמִן, and he certainly interpreted Abraham's life accordingly. Paul, on the other hand, linked Abram's faith to the second clause in Genesis 15:6 וַיַּחְשְׁבֶהָ לֹּוֹ צְדָקָה "and he considered it for him righteousness." This crediting is a simple past *wayyiqtol*, a complete act, including the endpoint. That was Paul's point, and his application of this verse fits the Hebrew, too.

There is another ambiguity with the word "him." Did Abram consider God's promise "righteous," or did God consider Abram's faithfulness "righteous"? There is a hint in Hebrew that God responded to Abram's faithfulness by considering it "righteousness." The language choices appear to track Abram as the main participant on stage. There is a little helping word "to him" that weaves through the story. In v. 1 the word of Yahweh comes "to Abram." In both 15:4 and 15:7 when Yahweh speaks to Abram, an extra pronoun is added for Abram, אֵלָיו ("to him"). The author was using Abram as the point of reference. This makes it probable that the phrase "to him" in 15:6 was referring to Abram: "and [the LORD] considered it [Abram's faithfulness] for him [Abram, a pronominal tracking device] righteousness." Incidentally, the medieval commentator Rashi (1040 – 1105) reads Genesis 15:6 similarly: הַקָּדוֹשׁ בָּרוּךְ הוּא חֲשָׁבָהּ לְאַבְרָם לִזְכוּת וְלִצְדָקָה עַל הָאֱמָנָה שֶׁהֶאֱמִין בּוֹ: "the Holy One, blessed be he, considered it for *Abram* merit and righteousness because of the faith that he placed in him."

Abraham is the father of faith. God is good and his promises are trustworthy. As we journey through life on earth, we do not always see God's perspective on individual situations, just like

Abraham did not see how he was going to have children and a great inheritance. But Abraham was trusting God. We can be encouraged. Our faith is not a one-time assertion, but a life of faithfulness. We may look back and say "we have believed God." More practically, we learn from this verse that we please God when we are trusting him. We are believing that his promises are true and sure in Jesus Christ so that we do not need to fear the future even if we do not know the future. We live and grow in faith.

Randall Buth

Emotional Meltdown: Stuttering in Hebrew

GENESIS 37:30b

MT	ESV
הַיֶּלֶד אֵינֶנּוּ וַאֲנִי אָנָה אֲנִי־בָא׃	The boy is gone, and I, where shall I go?

After convincing his brothers to leave Joseph in the pit, Reuben steps away from the group and misses the meal at which the brothers sell Joseph to the traveling Midianites (37:25–28). Reuben had planned to go back to the cistern secretly to rescue his youngest brother Joseph, but unbeknownst to him, the Midianites had bought him for twenty pieces of silver and took him down to Egypt to be sold as a slave. Unaware of these developments, Reuben hurries to the cistern and finds it empty! Overcome with despair and grief, Reuben spontaneously tears his clothes and utters a statement that could be construed as stuttering (involuntary repetitions of sounds), stammering (involuntary repetitions and hesitations in speech), or blubbering (uncontrollable noisy sobbing). Reuben no doubt assumes that Joseph is dead since his brothers had recently threatened to kill him. Reuben is overcome with grief and breaks out in a sharp and piercing outcry.

In this passage, the author intentionally combines two sound-related poetic devices — assonance (repeated vowels) and alliteration (repeated consonants) — to express the confused and emotional state of Reuben. The repetition of the vowel "a" and consonants א (*aleph*) and נ (*nun*) engulf the stuttered speech of Reuben. Although these literary devices are found primarily in poetry (e.g., Ps 147:13; Song 6:3; Isa 22:5; 24:17), narrative prose occasionally borrows the features in order to emphasize a point—in this case, confusion and grief.

Assonance and alliteration join a series of similar-sounding words into one key idea. They can also serve as mnemonic devices to assist in the memorization of a text, especially in an oral culture. By providing a vivid and sudden shift in the flow of the language, these two features highlight a critical juncture in the narrative and draw the reader further into the story. Hebrew pericopes that include assonance and alliteration are difficult to translate accurately into modern languages. Consequently, readers of modern translations often miss the intensity of the Reuben discourse and the emotional outburst expressed in the Hebrew language.

In our story, Reuben is at a loss for words. He is distraught, disturbed, confused, and angry. What would he do now that his brother was gone? What would his father do upon learning of the disappearance of his favorite son? Modern translators have attempted to represent the mood of this pericope, but none has succeeded in expressing the explosion of emotions released by Reuben, primarily because of the lack of linguistic equivalents between languages. When the reader of the pericope encounters the speech of Reuben laden with assonance and alliteration, he/she is immediately engulfed into his stuttering and emotional outcry. Reuben's utterance is not connected to the question of where he should go, as found in most modern translations: "The child is not; and I, whither shall I go?" (KJV); "The boy isn't there! And I, where can I go?" (NET); "The boy is gone; and I, where can I turn?" (NRSV); "The boy isn't there! Where can I turn now?" (NIV); rather, it is directly linked to his emotional state: "The boy's gone! What am I going to do!" (*The Message*);

"The boy is GONE! Oh no! Oh NO! NO! What am I going to do now??" (my translation).

Emotional outbursts and passionate feelings are a part of human nature. It should not surprise us that biblical characters expressed them vividly in their discourse! Moses (Exod 17:4), Job (3:11 – 16), David (Ps 42:11), and even Jesus (Matt 21:12) burst out with emotions. God welcomes our outbursts and assures us that none of them is beyond his control and sovereign rule over our lives.

Hélène Dallaire

God Prepares His Messengers

EXODUS 4:11

MT	ESV
וַיֹּאמֶר יְהוָה אֵלָיו מִי שָׂם פֶּה לָאָדָם	Then the LORD said to him, "Who has made man's mouth?
אוֹ מִי־יָשׂוּם אִלֵּם אוֹ חֵרֵשׁ	Who makes him mute, or deaf,
אוֹ פִקֵּחַ אוֹ עִוֵּר הֲלֹא אָנֹכִי יְהוָה:	or seeing, or blind? Is it not I, the LORD?"

Have you ever questioned your ministry ability? Moses, one of Israel's greatest leaders, did. The Lord of all creation selected and sent Moses on a mission to go to God's people and communicate his message. But the prophet was not a ready and willing messenger.

Scripture calls God's servants "messengers" (Mal 2:7) because God sends them. Moses reasons that he cannot be God's messenger, so he declines his assignment. His argument centers on his perceived inability, that he is unable to speak to his own satisfaction. Commentators speculate about the cause of Moses' inability. One thing is certain; God responds as if Moses' inability is a disability.

How do we know this? When Yahweh responds to Moses' refusal, he chooses words that illustrate his role in disabilities. In

Exodus 4:11 the words חֵרֵשׁ "deaf," אִלֵּם "mute," פִּקֵּחַ "sighted," and עִוֵּר "blind" all occur in the *piel*, indicating physical disabilities.[1] Because the four terms are uniquely inflected, this pattern plays a crucial role in interpreting this passage. It is particularly significant that the Hebrew word used here that our Bibles translate "mute" means "able to understand but not able to speak."[2] Because Moses comprehends the message, Yahweh challenges Moses to look beyond what he considers to be his speech limitations. Moses can understand; God will help him speak.

God patiently responds to Moses' logic when he asks him two questions: Who puts man's mouth in place? Who makes man unable to speak, hear, or see? Yes, remarkably, who makes those who cannot speak unable to speak? Wouldn't we expect God to say, "Who makes those unable to speak, able to speak?" But God's argument for Moses states that if Moses has a disability, God gave it to him. God should certainly have a fuller understanding of Moses' limitations than Moses did! This verse not only addresses God's role in disabilities, but it also sets the stage for his provision through his people.

In the prophets, God echoes his role in disability: "In that day, declares the LORD, I will assemble the lame, and gather the outcasts, and those whom I have afflicted" (Mic 4:6, ESV). Like Exodus 4:11, this passage reminds us that God assumes sovereign responsibility for disability, which includes assuring us that he will one day heal those who have disabilities. "The LORD gives sight to the blind" (Ps 146:8, NIV). For now, we may choose to say with Job, God's agent to assist people with disabilities, "I was eyes to the blind and feet to the lame" (Job 29:15, NIV).

If God calls us to speak, he will enable us to speak. For those of us who have a disability, as most of us will as we age, this passage assures us that God not only gives us our mission assignments, he also empowers us for the task. Disability should not keep us from experiencing the joy of serving God. What is more, our greatest joy in serving God may come from helping others with their disabilities.

Dave Deuel

Notes

1. C. L. Seow, *A Grammar for Biblical Hebrew* (Nashville: Abingdon, 1995), 21.

2. John I. Durham, *Exodus*, WBC 3 (Waco, TX: Word, 1987), 50. One translation renders the passage focusing on Yahweh's ability to enable or disable: "The LORD said to him, 'Who makes a man able to talk? Who makes him unable to hear or speak? Who makes him able to see? Who makes him blind? It is I, the LORD'" (Exod 4:11, NIrV).

You, Who, Me?

MT	NIV
לֹא תַעֲשֶׂה־לְךָ פֶסֶל	You shall not make for yourself an image
וְכָל־תְּמוּנָה אֲשֶׁר בַּשָּׁמַיִם מִמַּעַל	in the form of anything in heaven above
וַאֲשֶׁר בָּאָרֶץ מִתָּחַת	or on the earth beneath
וַאֲשֶׁר בַּמַּיִם מִתַּחַת לָאָרֶץ	or in the waters below.

What is often lost in translation is the real meaning of "you." In English, the personal pronoun "you" can be singular or plural. In other languages, "you-singular" and "you-plural" are clearly distinguished. In Spanish, for example, we have "usted" and "ustedes." In Chinese, we have 你 (nǐ) and 你們 (nǐ men). When it comes to the Ten Commandments, such as "You shall have no other gods before me," which "you" do we have?

Surprisingly, all the verbal forms and second person pronominal suffixes in the Decalogue are masculine singular. That is why Exodus 20:4a says לֹא תַעֲשֶׂה־לְךָ פֶסֶל, "You shall not make for yourself an image" (singular), and not the similar but plural construction as found in Deuteronomy 4:16a, פֶּן־תַּשְׁחִתוּן וַעֲשִׂיתֶם לָכֶם פֶּסֶל, "so that you do not become corrupt and make for yourselves an idol" (NIV). In other words, the Ten Commandments are not written to "you-plural" but to "you-singular." They are not written to "you all" but to "you" as an individual.

This is unusual in the context of the giving of the law on Mount Sinai in Exodus 19. The entire nation is gathered at the foot of the mountain to witness Yahweh speaking to Moses in a theophanic appearance of thunder, lightning, and smoke. God himself conveys to the Israelites through Moses, "You yourselves have seen what I did to Egypt, and how I carried you on eagles' wings and brought you to myself" (Exod 19:4), addressing them in the plural. One would expect the same plural address in the Decalogue.

The fact that the Ten Commandments are addressed to *you* in the singular emphasizes their personal and ethical character. It has long been observed that these statements are not "commandments" per se or even "laws." There are no specific punishments spelled out for breaking these "laws" as in the Book of the Covenant (Exod 21–23), and the tenth commandment, "You shall not covet…" is not even a law one can observably break! Rather, the Ten Commandments are ten principles for personal conduct in daily life, and they are just as relevant today as they were in the days of Moses.

As believers, we have not only made a commitment to the gospel of Christ, but we have made a commitment to a system of personal ethics inculcated in the eternal moral law of the Decalogue. These principles include exclusive worship, parental honor, respect for life, respect for the marriage bond, and respect for the personal property of others. George Mendenhall has put it well: the Ten Commandments should really be called the "Ten Commitments."[1]

Since the Ten Commitments are really a personal system of ethics and not corporate law—that is, they speak to the singular "you," not the plural "you"—they cannot be applied to corporate entities. The sixth commandment, "You shall not kill," for example, cannot be applied to corporate structures like governments and to such issues as capital punishment. Rather, the singular "you" emphasizes the personal nature of these commitments and the fact that one cannot hide in the shadows of a corporate body like the church. Our commitments must be singular and personal.

The old-time preachers used to say, "God has no grand-children." Each generation must make their own spiritual commitments afresh and anew. Faith cannot be inherited. Have *you*-singular made such a commitment? May our response never be, "Who, me?"

Milton Eng

Notes

1. George E. Mendenhall, *Ancient Israel's Faith and History: An Introduction to the Bible in Context*, ed. Gary A. Herion (Louisville: Westminster John Knox, 2001), 60–61.

How's Your Walk?

MT	ESV
אֶת־מִשְׁפָּטַי תַּעֲשׂוּ וְאֶת־חֻקֹּתַי תִּשְׁמְרוּ	You shall follow my rules and keep my statutes
לָלֶכֶת בָּהֶם אֲנִי יְהוָה אֱלֹהֵיכֶם׃	and walk in them. I am the LORD your God.

The ESV translates this verse with three parallel commands. Yet, the Hebrew text has only two finite verbs (imperatival *yiqtol*/imperfects), "follow" and "keep." The translation "walk," לָלֶכֶת, is an infinitive construct with the prefixed preposition לְ. Since the Hebrew construction does not attest three parallel imperatival forms as translated in the ESV, how does the infinitive construct relate to the two main finite verbs?

Finite verbs are "finite" because they are limited to a grammatical subject that can be the first, second, or third person. They also mark mood and tense-aspect. Nonfinite verbs (participles and infinitives) are not limited by person, but still carry some qualities of verbs. The actions of chief importance to the speaker are usually conveyed through the use of finite verbs; nonfinite verbs usually communicate subordinate ideas (participles are also used verbally to mark mood and tense-aspect).

The infinitive construct often functions much like the English infinitive. But Hebrew also has additional important functions that can challenge the translator. In Leviticus 18:4, one

27

option is to render the infinitive construct as a formal equivalent to the Hebrew, "to walk" (KJV, NASB). A reader may understand this to function as purpose or result, but how "following" and "keeping" find their purpose in "walking" is not obvious. Another option is to take the infinitive construct as nominal in the sense of complementary, i.e., completing the main verb תִּשְׁמְרוּ, "[you must] be careful to follow my decrees" (NIV), in which case the main idea becomes the walking ("to follow") instead of the watching ("be careful"), and the parallelism of the two finite verbs is lost. A third option is to mark the adverbial nature of the infinitive construct, "following them" (NRSV), without indicating which adverbial function is intended. All of these are viable.

Hebrew also uses the infinitive construct to convey functions such as time, means, manner, cause, concession, purpose, and result (cf. the adverbial participle in Greek). The precise function is often marked by a preceding preposition. Joined to the infinitive construct, the most flexible of the Hebrew prepositions — and therefore most imprecise — is the לְ, as is employed in our verse here; knowing this can open up options beyond purpose.

The לְ + infinitive construct has at least three possible adverbial functions: manner, concession, and result. A good example of the function of manner is found in Exodus 20:8, "Remember the Sabbath day *by* keeping [לְ + infinitive construct] it holy" (NIV, italics added). In Leviticus 18:4, the function of manner likewise makes good sense: "You shall follow my rules and keep my statutes *by* walking in them." First, this understanding preserves the finite verbs, the imperatives "follow" and "keep," as the main verbs and the infinitive construct as a subordinate idea. Second, the infinitive construct can now modify both main verbs. Third, translating the לְ + infinitive construct with the phrase "*by* walking" clarifies how one is to carry out the two commands.

Leviticus 18 is one of the more "adult" chapters of the Bible.

The first five verses introduce the topic by giving the general principle of how important it is not to practice the lifestyles of the Egyptians or the Canaanites but to obey Yahweh's commands. In this chapter, Yahweh commands that his people demonstrate this difference in the realm of sexuality. English and Hebrew both use walking as a metaphor for behavior. Here in this most fundamental characteristic of human life, sexuality, our lives should stand in stark contrast to those who do not worship Yahweh. It may seem redundant, but Leviticus 18:4 emphasizes that the way we obey the instructions of Yahweh is not mere lip service; it is in how we actually conduct ourselves. This is especially true in the area of sexuality.

Lee M. Fields

Productive and Protected Ministry

NUMBERS 17:23 [ENGLISH 17:8]

MT	NIV
וַיְהִי מִמָּחֳרָת	The next day
וַיָּבֹא מֹשֶׁה אֶל־אֹהֶל הָעֵדוּת	Moses entered the tent
וְהִנֵּה פָּרַח מַטֵּה־אַהֲרֹן	and saw that Aaron's staff,
לְבֵית לֵוִי	which represented the tribe of Levi,
וַיֹּצֵא פֶרַח	had not only sprouted but had budded,
וַיָּצֵץ צִיץ	blossomed
וַיִּגְמֹל שְׁקֵדִים׃	and produced almonds.

Complaining against the leadership of Moses and Aaron, which constituted rebellion against God, had cost many Israelite lives (Num 16:1 – 17:15 [Eng. 16:1 – 50]). So Yahweh set up a definitive test to end such grumbling by miraculously demonstrating his choice of a high priest: "The staff belonging to the man I choose will sprout [פרח]" (Num 17:20 [17:5]). Sure enough, of the staffs belonging to tribal chieftains, only Aaron's responded to God's choice. Not only did it sprout, but it bore (וַיִּגְמֹל) ripened almonds overnight! In wonder at the cumulative effects of the Creator's touch, the Hebrew text bursts into a rapturous crescendo of poetic parallelism with alliteration (repetition of צ; 17:23 [17:8]).

This miracle linked Aaron to the high priestly office in two ways. First, the staff on which his name was inscribed put forth almond buds/blossoms (פֶּרַח), just as the lamps in the tabernacle, which the high priest tended, were "shaped like almond flowers with buds and blossoms (פֶּרַח)" (Exod 25:33–4; 37:19–20). Second, the word צִיץ refers to the (collective) "blossoms" produced by Aaron's staff, and elsewhere the same term is used for the rosette that decorated the front of the high priest's turban (Exod 28:36; 39:30; Lev 8:9).

"The LORD said to Moses, 'Put back Aaron's staff in front of the ark of the covenant law, to be kept as a sign to the rebellious. This will put an end to their grumbling against me, so that they will not die'" (17:25 [17:10]). Aaron's staff would serve as a warning, but the demonstration seems too benign for that purpose ... unless we recognize an additional connection in the Hebrew.

Why almonds? There is no evidence that Aaron's rod was made of almond wood. Nor did Hebrew have the expression, "You're driving me nuts!" However, the word for "almond" (שָׁקֵד) is derived from the same root as the verb for "keep watch, be awake, be vigilant" (שקד). This is because the almond tree is "watchful/awake" in the sense that it is the first tree to blossom every year while other trees continue their winter slumber. Now we can understand, for example, God's object lesson to young Jeremiah, which otherwise does not make sense in English: "'What do you see, Jeremiah?' 'I see the branch of an almond tree [שָׁקֵד],' I replied. The LORD said to me, 'You have seen correctly, for I am watching [participle of שקד] to see that my word is fulfilled'" (Jer 1:11–12).

Aaron's almonds implied watchfulness to guard his priesthood. Any rebel would be apprehended by the vigilant deity who never sleeps (Ps 121:4), whose watchful almond-blossom-shaped lamps provided light in his tabernacle through every night (Exod 27:21; Lev 24:3).

Aaron's staff was not inherently better than other wooden sticks. Nor was Aaron inherently better than other Israelites. After all, he had been responsible for making the golden calf (Exod 32:2–4, 24)! But God's choice made him fruitful and protected his ministry. Similarly, God has chosen all who believe in his Son, faulty as we are: "But you are a chosen people, a royal priesthood, a holy nation, a people belonging to God, that you may declare the praises of him who called you out of darkness into his wonderful light" (1 Pet 2:9). Like Aaron, we can be assured that God will guard our service for him and make it productive.

Roy E. Gane

All Your *Lēbāb*

MT	NIV
שְׁמַע יִשְׂרָאֵל יְהוָה אֱלֹהֵינוּ יְהוָה אֶחָד׃	[4] Hear, O Israel: The LORD our God, the LORD is one.
וְאָהַבְתָּ אֵת יְהוָה אֱלֹהֶיךָ בְּכָל־לְבָבְךָ וּבְכָל־נַפְשְׁךָ וּבְכָל־מְאֹדֶךָ׃	[5] Love the LORD your God with all your heart (לֵבָב) and with all your soul and with all your strength.
וְהָיוּ הַדְּבָרִים הָאֵלֶּה אֲשֶׁר אָנֹכִי מְצַוְּךָ הַיּוֹם עַל־לְבָבֶךָ׃	[6] These commandments that I give you today are to be on your hearts (לֵבָב).
וְשִׁנַּנְתָּם לְבָנֶיךָ וְדִבַּרְתָּ בָּם בְּשִׁבְתְּךָ בְּבֵיתֶךָ וּבְלֶכְתְּךָ בַדֶּרֶךְ וּבְשָׁכְבְּךָ וּבְקוּמֶךָ׃	[7] Impress them on your children. Talk about them when you sit at home and when you walk along the road, when you lie down and when you get up.
וּקְשַׁרְתָּם לְאוֹת עַל־יָדֶךָ וְהָיוּ לְטֹטָפֹת בֵּין עֵינֶיךָ׃	[8] Tie them as symbols on your hands and bind them on your foreheads.
וּכְתַבְתָּם עַל־מְזוּזֹת בֵּיתֶךָ וּבִשְׁעָרֶיךָ׃	[9] Write them on the doorframes of your houses and on your gates.

The law of Moses, the Torah, is the foundation of the Old Testament. Deuteronomy is the summation of the Torah, and this passage is the heart of Deuteronomy. Built on the confession that Yahweh alone is our God, it calls us to respond to him with wholehearted love, to be purposeful and diligent to remember his words, and to pass them on to the next generation.

The New Testament repeats the call to love in three variations: Matthew 22:37; Mark 12:30; and Luke 10:27. Deuteronomy and Matthew each have three elements, but Matthew does not include "strength" and appears to add "mind." Mark and Luke have four elements, including both "strength" and "mind," though in different order.

These variations come from the Hebrew word לֵבָב. It is often translated in English as "heart." The Greek renders it as καρδία (also "heart"), but the New Testament writers do not limit the translation of לֵבָב to "heart." Rather, each reference also includes the Greek term διάνοια ("mind").

English speakers often distinguish between "heart knowledge" and "head knowledge," but in biblical Hebrew, לֵבָב refers to both the "heart" and the "mind" (and can further indicate "thinking," "feeling," or one's "will"). To be called to love Yahweh with all our לֵבָב implies not only our heartfelt devotion but also our thinking.

To live out this devotion to God, Moses tells the people to have Yahweh's words on their לֵבָב. While this does imply memorization, the point is that they should have these words *on their mind* in daily life. The English expression really is fitting. Like a tune we can't get out of our heads, or something we can't take off our minds, Moses instructs us to be deliberate about thinking on God's Word—to be so occupied with the word of Yahweh that we are in a sense preoccupied with it, so much so that it spills out in our words and actions.

If God's words are on our minds in this way, obeying the next command flows out from it. The verb שׁנן only occurs here and it appears in the *piel*, a verbal stem that may function to denote frequency. It is likely, then, that the verb שָׁנַן conveys the need to repeatedly instruct our children. Context supports this by listing venues for talking to our children (when we sit, walk, lie down, and get up). These show that we need to be talking with our children about God's Word throughout the day and from day to day. Failure to do this during the period of the judges meant many Israelite generations were largely lost to the covenant faith and/or paid a tough penalty. Failure to do this well today, or giving more place to other voices in our children's lives, can also lead to the failure to pass on meaningful faith to our children.

Brian L. Webster

Blessed (בָּרוּךְ) or Blessed (אַשְׁרֵי) or Both?

DEUTERONOMY 7:14a AND PSALM 128:1

MT		ESV
בָּרוּךְ תִּהְיֶה מִכָּל־הָעַמִּים	Deut 7:14a	You shall be blessed above all peoples.
אַשְׁרֵי כָּל־יְרֵא יְהוָה הַהֹלֵךְ בִּדְרָכָיו׃	Ps 128:1	Blessed is everyone who fears the LORD, who walks in his ways!

Pervasive in our culture is the idea that "to be blessed" is to have abundance. We live in a culture that values things and considers them blessings. Scripture presents a picture that differs greatly from this Western mindset. In the Beatitudes (Matt 5:3–12), for example, we read that those who are "blessed" are the poor in spirit, those who mourn, the meek, those who hunger and thirst for righteousness, the merciful, the pure in heart, the peacemakers, and those who are persecuted for righteousness's sake. None of these speak of earthly blessings. Rather, they speak of the condition of the heart.

In English versions of the Bible, two Hebrew words are translated "blessed": בָּרוּךְ and אַשְׁרֵי. The word בָּרוּךְ appears frequently in contexts where humans bless God by giving him praise (Gen 9:26; 14:20; 24:27; Exod 18:10; 1 Sam 24:32; 2 Sam 22:47; 1 Kgs 1:48; Ps 28:6). Some have suggested that the term is connected to the word for "knee" (בֶּרֶךְ), implying that the worshiper comes before God in a posture of humility to bless him on bended knee. The word בָּרוּךְ also appears in contexts where God blesses his children (e.g., Abraham, Isaac, Israel, Gad, Samuel, Abigail, David, men of Jabesh Gilead, Solomon, Boaz, Ruth). Someone blessed (בָּרוּךְ) by God is empowered with divine favor for a specific purpose.

The word אַשְׁרֵי, often rendered "happy" or "blessed," describes the state of a believer whose walk with God is noticeably honorable and righteous. The term is never used for God; it only applies to humans. The individual who is אַשְׁרֵי is identified as one who lives uprightly before God (Pss 106:3; 119:1; Isa 56:2), sets his/her hope in him (Pss 34:9; 146:5; Isa 30:18), listens to wisdom (1 Kgs 10:8; 2 Chr 9:7; Prov 3:13), abstains from evil (Pss 1:1; 40:5), trusts in Yahweh (Pss 2:12; 40:5[4]; 89:16[15]), receives forgiveness from Yahweh (Ps 32:1), acts justly (Isa 56:1), takes refuge in God (Pss 2:12; 34:9[8]), helps the poor (Ps 41:2[1]; Prov 14:21), walks in the light of Yahweh (Ps 89:16[15]), receives discipline from him (Ps 94:12; Job 5:17), delights in his commandments (Ps 112:1), fears Yahweh (Ps 128:1–2) and seeks him with his/her whole heart (Ps 119:2; Prov 8:34).

The state of "blessedness" of the individual who is אַשְׁרֵי is a result of ongoing righteous living. Consequently, it is reserved for those whose lives are wholeheartedly committed to God. There is nothing superficial or light about being אַשְׁרֵי. It describes a state that is far beyond human happiness and blessedness. The one who is אַשְׁרֵי is to be envied, to be followed, and to be a model in life, as he/she follows God.

As Christians, we are blessed beyond measure (בָּרוּךְ and אַשְׁרֵי) not because we have possessions, prestige, or power, but rather because we walk humbly with the living God— the Creator of heaven and earth. The blessings we receive from him are exceedingly abundant, above all we could ever ask. They are more than anything the world could offer, more than any happiness material things could bring, and more than any human could ever provide. As those who fear Yahweh and seek to walk uprightly before him, may our lives reflect the light of Yahweh and serve as a beacon to draw all people to him. To him be the glory!

Hélène Dallaire

A Challenging Commission

MT	NASB
רַק חֲזַק וֶאֱמַץ מְאֹד	Only be strong and very courageous;
לִשְׁמֹר לַעֲשׂוֹת כְּכָל־הַתּוֹרָה	Be careful to do according to all the law
אֲשֶׁר צִוְּךָ מֹשֶׁה עַבְדִּי	which Moses My servant commanded you;
אַל־תָּסוּר מִמֶּנּוּ יָמִין וּשְׂמֹאול	do not turn from it to the right or to the left,
לְמַעַן תַּשְׂכִּיל בְּכֹל אֲשֶׁר תֵּלֵךְ׃	so that you may have success wherever you go.

It is tempting to reduce Israel's campaign in Canaan to military terms. Strength and courage, as well as speed and cunning, are attributes of value in a contest of arms. These ideas rush to mind when one encounters God's command to Joshua: חֲזַק וֶאֱמַץ, "Be strong and courageous."

However, a closer read reveals something else. In the context, the campaign is essentially a pedestrian one. To be successful, Israel's feet must follow the leader and tread ground (cf. 1:2–3). God goes before his people in word (2:10) and symbol (cf. 3:11). Any reordering of matters will court disaster. Accordingly, the narrative frames Israel's challenge not in terms of knuckle-busting power, but in terms of careful obedience.

Consider the driving idea launched in speeches from Moab. Subordinate to the command to "be strong and very courageous" is a pair of infinitive constructs, לִשְׁמֹר לַעֲשׂוֹת, "to keep on doing" or "to cautiously keep." These modify the command and give it specific direction. The weight of this entire verbal chain, therefore, bears down on a single object: כְּכָל־הַתּוֹרָה. How this changes everything! While strength and courage are needed when gripping a sword or throwing a spear, this is hardly the concern here. God directs Joshua to be fierce in keeping *all the Torah*. The people later echo this same concern (1:18).

Perhaps the meaning of this is better appreciated when the imperatives of the section are aligned with their opposites. The opposite of being strong and courageous (1:6, 7, 9) is being weak and timid. The opposite of being careful (1:7) is being sloppy, and the opposite of being meditative (1:8) is being thoughtless. Between these poles of choice lay the true challenge of the conquest. Will Israel be strong, courageous, careful, and meditative in handling Torah? Or will Israel be weak, timid, sloppy, and thoughtless in handling Torah? The stakes are enormous.

That this future is truly a choice and not some deal where blessings are automatically dispensed is also suggested. The particle רַק stands at the head of v. 7 and introduces a note of contingency. For his part, God promises land to Israel. For Israel's part, the duty of obedience must stand: *only* be very strong and courageous."

Beyond this particle, one other term requires a closer look. The verb translated "you will be successful," תַּשְׂכִּיל, is drawn from a wisdom tradition and is translated elsewhere with the idea of "prudence" or "understanding." The root is used again in 1:8, but there is preceded by תַּצְלִיחַ, "you will prosper." This act is often achieved by pressing, choosing well, or chopping through. Taken together, these terms suggest that choosing the "strong and courageous" route means tenaciously following a well-defined road to a true understanding, one that appreciates the rightful place of God's grace and human duty in life. The "weak and timid" route, by contrast, is connected to deviation and misunderstanding.

Lurking in the shadow of the latter are ominous precedents: the record of Israel's rebellion in the wilderness, the recitation of "curses for disobedience" ordered by Moses, and the prediction of future failure. The charge of God at the start of Joshua's campaign is a challenging commission. It orients the careful reader to consider the narrative that follows not in terms of military prowess, but in terms of faithful obedience. Such obedience to his will is what God wants of us as well.

Mark Ziese

Rahab's Hope

MT	ESV
הִנֵּה אֲנַחְנוּ בָאִים בָּאָרֶץ	Behold, when we come into the land,
אֶת־תִּקְוַת חוּט הַשָּׁנִי הַזֶּה תִּקְשְׁרִי בַּחַלּוֹן	you shall tie this scarlet cord in the window
אֲשֶׁר הוֹרַדְתֵּנוּ בוֹ	through which you let us down,
	and you shall gather into your house
וְאֶת־אָבִיךְ וְאֶת־אִמֵּךְ וְאֶת־אַחַיִךְ	your father and mother, your brothers,
וְאֵת כָּל־בֵּית אָבִיךְ	and all your father's household.[1]
תַּאַסְפִי אֵלַיִךְ הַבָּיְתָה:	

Joshua's two spies, or "the messengers" (הַמַּלְאָכִים), as they are called in 6:17, 25, were treated hospitably by Rahab the prostitute. When the men of the city demanded she hand them over, she sent the men away to pursue a false path, while the two "messengers" escaped. The city was then utterly destroyed, and only Rahab and her family escaped.

Why would they be called "messengers"? They had no message. Perhaps the term is meant to help connect this story with the two "angels" whom Lot entertained (Gen 19:1, הַמַּלְאָכִים).

There are many parallels between these stories. Like Rahab, Lot was hospitable in an otherwise hostile city. Men vainly pursued the spies and the angels all night. Lot and Rahab both escaped doomed cities with their kin. Both cities fell by divine intervention. The Israelite attack under Joshua did to Jericho what the heavenly host did to Sodom. Thus, by rendering judgment against Jericho, Joshua and Israel imaged the divine assembly.

Speaking of Genesis, there is another "prostitute" there with a red cord. Judah mistook Tamar for a shrine prostitute (Gen 38:15). When she birthed twins, she marked her firstborn, Zerah, with a red cord (38:27–30). In Joshua, the red cord marks the first fruit of the land, i.e., the first city to be taken for Yahweh. The firstborn and the first fruit are for God, marked in red.

Regarding the firstborn, the "destroyer" took the firstborn of Egypt, except those marked with blood (Exod 12:23). Rahab's red cord serves the same function, when another destroyer, namely Joshua, passed over her house. This was Rahab's Passover. Of course, Christ, who is our Passover (1 Cor 5:7), saves us from death. Because of his blood we will be passed over when Jesus, the last Joshua, comes with his angels/messengers to judge the world.

Note that תִּקְוָה is glossed "rope" only here. Everywhere else in the Hebrew Bible (over thirty times) it means "hope" or "positive expectation." Is this double entendre? The red cord symbolizes her hope of deliverance, her confidence in a future with the people of Yahweh. "For God alone, O my soul, wait in silence, for my hope [תִּקְוָה] is from him" (Ps 62:5, ESV). The verb "to bind" (קשׁר) when followed by the בְ preposition can be used metaphorically, as in, "Folly is bound up in the heart of a child" (Prov 22:15, ESV); or "Bind them on your heart always" (Prov 6:21a, ESV). What then does Joshua 2:18 connote? "Bind on the window the hope signified by this scarlet thread." Christ's blood, which covers us from the guilt of sin, is our hope.

The verb "bind" also can mean "to conspire against."

Rahab's secret hope of salvation with its symbol of the red cord, her Passover experience, is executed in a conspiratorial way, unbeknownst to the rulers of her doomed city.

Could the verse really imply all that? Can a Christian see in it both the plain meaning of the text and an element of salvation from death in Jesus' blood? Or should we just pick one sense and leave it at that?

George Schwab

Notes

1. Please note that the fourth line in English is the last line in Hebrew. To read the second Hebrew line, start with the second-to-last word (the verb) and work backward more or less, concluding with "in the window," the last Hebrew word in the line.

Who Saved Israel, Othniel or Yahweh?

JUDGES 3:9

MT	NIV
וַיִּזְעֲקוּ בְנֵי־יִשְׂרָאֵל אֶל־יְהוָה	But when [the Israelites] cried out to the LORD,
וַיָּקֶם יְהוָה מוֹשִׁיעַ לִבְנֵי יִשְׂרָאֵל	he raised up for them a deliverer,
וַיּוֹשִׁיעֵם אֵת עָתְנִיאֵל בֶּן־קְנַז אֲחִי כָלֵב הַקָּטֹן מִמֶּנּוּ׃	Othniel son of Kenaz, Caleb's younger brother, who saved them.

You may recall the theme that summarizes Israel's life before God in the book of Judges, "In those days there was no king in Israel. Everyone did what was right in his own eyes." (Judg 17:6 ESV; cf. 18:1; 19:1; 21:25). This period in Israel's history was not one characterized by covenant keeping and faithfulness. In fact, it was the opposite. Israel repeatedly lapsed into cycles of infidelity, a cycle summarized in Judges 2:11 – 19: (1) the Israelites did evil in the eyes of Yahweh; (2) Yahweh sold them into the hands of foreign oppressors; (3) the Israelites cried out to Yahweh for help; (4) Yahweh raised up a judge to deliver Israel; (5) the land had rest; (6) the judge died; and then the cycle began all over again. Sound familiar?

The first judge raised up by Yahweh, identified in 3:9, was

Othniel, from the tribe of Judah. As the first judge, he becomes the standard by which all subsequent judges are measured.

This verse consists of three verbal clauses, each of which begins with an imperfect verb prefixed with the *waw* consecutive: Israel cried out, Yahweh raised up, and then he saved them. The question is, who is "he"? Who saved Israel, Othniel or Yahweh? The translations appear to complicate the issue. The NIV is representative (cf. KJV, RSV, ESV, NASB, NET).

In the first two verbal clauses, the subjects are explicit, even though the translation leaves them out, "the children of Israel" cried out and "Yahweh" raised up. In the third verbal clause, however, the verbal subject is implied, meaning that it must be determined from context. All of the translations appear to suggest that the subject of the verb וַיּוֹשִׁיעֵם in line three is Othniel — that is, "Othniel, who saved them." The problem with these translations, however, is that they do not follow the grammar of the text.

Consider that the identification of Othniel in line three is preceded by the particle אֵת. This particle can be interpreted in one of two ways, either as the Hebrew preposition "with," or as the untranslatable definite direct object marker, also known as the accusative particle. Since the object of the verb clearly appears as the 3mp pronominal suffix on the verb ("he saved them"), the particle אֵת is best interpreted as the preposition meaning "with." In other words, the implied subject of the verb in the third clause is not Othniel, but Yahweh. Consider the following revised translation of Judges 3:9:

> "Then the children of Israel cried out to Yahweh,
> and so Yahweh raised up a deliverer
> for the children of Israel,
> and he [Yahweh] saved them with Othniel the
> son of Kenaz, Caleb's younger brother."

In this revised translation an important distinction present in Hebrew is made clear: Yahweh is identified as the agent of Israel's salvation while Othniel becomes the instrument by which Yahweh saves. Careful grammatical analysis and clear translations are fundamental to good theology. While Yahweh may use human instruments to deliver his people, just as he did with the judges, we must never forget that it is always Yahweh who saves (cf. Judg 2:18; 6:36, 37; 7:7; 10:12). We must never forget to distinguish between the instruments and the agent of our great salvation.

Miles V. Van Pelt

Hannah's Request

I SAMUEL I:28

MT	NIV
וְגַם אָנֹכִי הִשְׁאִלְתִּהוּ לַיהוָה	"So now I give him to the LORD.
כָּל־הַיָּמִים אֲשֶׁר הָיָה הוּא שָׁאוּל לַיהוָה	For his whole life he will be given over to the LORD."
וַיִּשְׁתַּחוּ שָׁם לַיהוָה׃	And he worshiped the LORD there.

Have you ever prayed and asked God for something? When we make our prayer requests, we usually want to *keep* what we've asked from God. How many of us would pray for something and then give it right back to God? Hannah did just that. She made a vow: if God would grant her a son, she would give him back to God (1 Sam 1:11). Why would she do that?

Hannah appears in 1 Samuel 1 and 2. The book of 1 Samuel recounts the history of Israel in its transitional time, from the period of the judges to the establishment of a monarchy. Samuel is a judge, a priest, and a prophet. It is Samuel who anointed the first king of Israel, Saul, and later he also anointed David. The story begins with Samuel's mother, Hannah, in order to show the subsequent kings of Israel that God desires obedience more than sacrifice or offering (see 15:22). Hannah prayed for a son. She feared that God would forget her by rejecting her requests (1:11). Through God's granting of a son, Hannah experienced God's grace. In fact, the name "Hannah" (חַנָּה) means "grace"

(חֵן). Out of gratitude to God, Hannah willingly gives her son back to God.

For Hannah, giving Samuel back to God is not an afterthought, emphasized by the different uses of a single verb, שׁאל, meaning both "request" and "give" (NIV). "Request" is the basic meaning of the root in the *qal* stem whereas "give back" is the meaning in the *hiphil* stem. When Hannah asked a son from God, she was already prepared to give him back to God. The root meaning "request" (שָׁאַל) occurs seven times in 1 Samuel 1 (1:17, 20, 20, 27, 27, 28 [2x]), and in fact forms a major theme in the book. The names of the two major characters of the book, Samuel and Saul, both contain the letters for the root word "request" or "ask." The name "Samuel" (שְׁמוּאֵל) could mean "the name of God" or "asked of God." The name "Saul" (שָׁאוּל) means "asked of."

Interestingly, both names in part appear in the same verse in 1 Samuel 1:28. The author of the book uses a wordplay, first by stating Hannah will give Samuel back to the Lord (הִשְׁאִלְתִּהוּ). Then he repeats the same phrase with a *qal* passive participle "give over," which is the exact word for Saul's name (שָׁאוּל). Here the author is subtly forming a contrast between Hannah's request and the Israelites' request for a king. Hannah's request is Godcentered. The Israelites' request is humancentered. By asking for a king, God said they rejected him (8:7).

Hannah's request is not simply a request. It is a devotion to God out of gratitude. Hannah's request is not just to get something from God, but to offer back to God what he has given to her. In other words, Hannah's request is an act of worship. Because of her sincere faith, God blessed her with five more children (1 Sam 2:21), and her first son, Samuel, became Israel's kingmaker.

Hannah's example reminds us to ask not just for our own self-serving purposes, but also as an act of worship to give back to God what we asked for.

Chloe Sun

A Fresh Look at the David and Goliath Story

I SAMUEL 17:1

MT	NASB
וַיַּאַסְפוּ פְלִשְׁתִּים אֶת־מַחֲנֵיהֶם לַמִּלְחָמָה וַיֵּאָסְפוּ שֹׂכֹה אֲשֶׁר	Now the Philistines gathered their armies for battle; and they were gathered at Socoh which
לִיהוּדָה וַיַּחֲנוּ בֵּין־שׂוֹכֹה	belongs to Judah, and they camped between Socoh and
וּבֵין־עֲזֵקָה בְּאֶפֶס דַּמִּים׃	Azekah, in Ephes Dammim.

A thorough knowledge of the Hebrew language and Israel's geography has significantly informed my understanding of many biblical accounts. When Bible readers combine their understanding of Hebrew with their understanding of geography, they gain valuable insight into the biblical text.

I remember reading the David and Goliath story as a boy and marveling at how God's power helped David win the battle. But the battle is about much more than a shepherd boy overcoming a giant; Israel's very existence as a nation was at stake!

The geography of the land informs the story. If the Philistines advanced much farther up the valley of Elah, they could travel the ridge route to Bethlehem, thereby establishing for themselves a foothold along the major north-south highway. To the south lay Hebron, and to the north lay Gibeah, Saul's capital. If the

Philistines took these cities, Israel was effectively finished. Saul had to stop them and he knew it, so his forces drew up in battle array to block the Philistine advance.

The writers of the Old Testament assumed their readers knew the lay of the land. Today, someone might ask, "Why doesn't the text tell us how serious the situation was?" It does; it tells us the Philistines were at Socoh. If United States citizens heard a news report announcing a foreign army had captured Washington, D.C., the news correspondent would not have to add, "This is a bad thing for the USA." Its people would all know, because they know Washington, D.C. is the nation's capital.

Some translations also miss an important clue in the Hebrew as to the battle's location. Two different Hebrew words for "valley" appear; the first, עֵמֶק ("valley of Elah," 17:2 NASB), denotes a broad, flat valley; the second, גַּיְא ("with the valley between them," 17:3 NASB) denotes a sharply sloped and narrow valley — "a ravine" (HCSB). Thus, while the valley of Elah is broad and spacious, it only pinches together in a few spaces — thus narrowing the choices for possible battle sites. Translations that render both Hebrew words "valley" miss the clue the narrator is providing for the battle's precise location.

Furthermore, 1 Samuel 17:4 says Goliath initially "came out" or "came forth" (יצא) from the Philistine camp. But as David arrived, Goliath was literally "coming up" (עלה), not coming out (17:23, 25 NIV). Many translations gloss over this difference, but perhaps the writer was trying to convey something. I suggest he was; Goliath was likely ascending the Israelite side of the ravine (17:3), taunting Saul's forces. This understanding of the text would explain why the text says, "The men of Israel ... fled from him" (17:24 NASB). Why would they flee, unless his coming up their side of the ravine made them fear his direct attack? If he stood out in the middle of the valley, they might be afraid, but they had no need to flee.

The David and Goliath story is one familiar to all of us. Yet, study of the Hebrew language and Israel's geography provides important insight as to the seriousness of Israel's situation, the exact location of the battle within the valley, and the dynamics of Goliath's taunting Israel's army. Understanding these elements reveals a depth to the story previously hidden.

Bryan Beyer

So He Will Be Struck Down and Die

2 SAMUEL 11:15

MT	NIV
וַיִּכְתֹּב בַּסֵּפֶר לֵאמֹר הָבוּ אֶת־אוּרִיָּה אֶל־מוּל פְּנֵי הַמִּלְחָמָה הַחֲזָקָה וְשַׁבְתֶּם מֵאַחֲרָיו וְנִכָּה וָמֵת׃	In it he wrote, "Put Uriah in the front line where the fighting is fiercest. Then withdraw from him so he will be struck down and die."

David is desperate. His attempt to cover up his adulterous affair with Uriah's wife, Bathsheba, has failed. When Bathsheba told him she was pregnant, David immediately orders Uriah back from the front lines and tries to get him (twice) to sleep with his wife. Uriah would then think the baby was his, conceived during his brief leave. But Uriah doesn't cooperate. He refuses to enjoy the comforts of home while Joab and the army are fighting Israel's enemies on the front lines. So David implements plan B; Uriah will have to die. David sends a message to Joab, ordering him to put Uriah on the front lines so he will "be struck down and die."

David's use of this expression, which combines the verbs נכה, "strike down," and מות, "die," is shocking, not simply because of its calloused disregard for Uriah's life, but because the expression appears elsewhere in the David story. David used this same combination of verbs when he described how he would "strike" and "kill" (וְהִכִּתִיו וַהֲמִיתִּיו) wild animals that threatened his sheep (1 Sam 17:35). The narrator then uses it when telling how David "struck down the Philistine and killed him" (וַיַּךְ אֶת־הַפְּלִשְׁתִּי וַיְמִיתֵהוּ, 1 Sam 17:50). "Striking" and "killing" is what David did to dangerous enemies of his flock and his people Israel (see also 2 Sam 10:18). Yet here he is plotting to have loyal Uriah, one of his best soldiers (23:39), struck down and killed. Rather than looking like the hero who struck down and killed Goliath, David now looks more like the cold-blooded assassins who have appeared in the prior stories. One of these was Joab, who struck down Abner so that he died (וַיַּכֵּהוּ שָׁם הַחֹמֶשׁ וַיָּמָת, 3:27). The NIV translates: "Joab stabbed [נכה] him in the stomach, and he died [מות]." Two other assassins, Rekab and Baanah, struck down and killed an innocent Ishbosheth (וַיַּכֻּהוּ וַיְמִתֻהוּ, 4:7).

The expression appears later in David's story as well. David's son Absalom decides to kill his half-brother Amnon to avenge his rape of Absalom's sister, Tamar. As he gives his henchmen their orders, he tells them to "strike down" and "kill" Amnon (הַכּוּ אֶת־אַמְנוֹן וַהֲמַתֶּם אֹתוֹ, 2 Sam 13:28). We are then told: "So Absalom's men did to Amnon what Absalom had ordered" (v. 29). This reverberation of David's crime suggests that the son is repeating his father's crime and contributes to the theme of poetic justice. The expression appears one more time, as the narrator describes how Joab's (how ironic!) men "struck" Absalom "and killed him" (וַיַּכּוּ אֶת־אַבְשָׁלוֹם וַיְמִיתֻהוּ, 18:15). Again, the theme of poetic justice emerges—Absalom gets what he dished out to Amnon, and David's command to strike down Uriah echoes in the account of his favorite son's violent death.

This survey of the collocation of two Hebrew verbs illustrates the importance of paying attention to verbal repetition in the text, for it is often the vehicle for thematic development. In this case, the repetition draws attention to the transformation that has come over David because of his fascination with lust and power. The great champion of Israel has now joined the ranks of its most vile criminals. The repetition also highlights God's justice. We do indeed reap what we sow.

Robert B. Chisholm Jr.

Understanding a Mother's Heart

I KINGS 3:25–26

MT	ESV
וַיֹּאמֶר הַמֶּלֶךְ גִּזְרוּ אֶת־הַיֶּלֶד הַחַי לִשְׁנָיִם וּתְנוּ אֶת־הַחֲצִי לְאַחַת וְאֶת־הַחֲצִי לְאֶחָת׃	25 And the king said, "Divide the living child in two, and give half to the one and half to the other."
וַתֹּאמֶר הָאִשָּׁה אֲשֶׁר־בְּנָהּ הַחַי אֶל־הַמֶּלֶךְ כִּי־נִכְמְרוּ רַחֲמֶיהָ עַל־בְּנָהּ וַתֹּאמֶר בִּי אֲדֹנִי תְּנוּ־לָהּ אֶת־הַיָּלוּד הַחַי וְהָמֵת אַל־תְּמִיתֻהוּ וְזֹאת אֹמֶרֶת גַּם־לִי גַם־לָךְ לֹא יִהְיֶה גְּזֹרוּ׃	26 Then the woman whose son was alive said to the king, because her heart yearned for her son, "Oh, my lord, give her the living child, and by no means put him to death." But the other said, "He shall be neither mine nor yours; divide him."

First Kings 3:16 begins the story of two disreputable prostitutes who bring their appeal for justice directly to the king. Solomon's great wisdom cuts through the lies and deception to discover the real mother. According to biblical law, decisions could be determined on the basis of the witness of two people, but here it was clearly one woman's word against another's. In the absence of other witnesses, there was no way to determine the legitimacy of either woman's claim. Nevertheless, God had gifted Solomon with unusual wisdom, and, as he anticipated, the true mother betrayed her love in her self-sacrificing plea to let the child live. It is here that English translations have difficulty conveying some of the nuances of the Hebrew.

For example, the depth of compassionate love the true mother demonstrated for her son is expressed in the plural form of "compassion" (רַחֲמֶיהָ, lit., "her compassions"). This is most likely an intensive plural[1] demonstrating a natural transition from the literal רֶחֶם ("womb") being the place of protection and comfort for a defenseless infant, to "compassion," the intense love for another. This plural form of the noun "compassion" is used three times with the *niphal* verb form of כמר (lit., "to grow hot, burn") to represent an emphatic way of saying "to move one to great compassion" (Gen 43:30; Hos 11:8). In the present case, her motherly compassion moved her to spare the child's life by giving him to the other woman, even though it meant that she would have to surrender her right to rear her precious child. In an attempt to capture the intensity of her emotion, the NIV is probably the most accurate. It states she "was deeply moved out of love for her son" (1 Kgs 3:26). By contrast, the surrogate mother would enjoy the benefits of having a child and yet lacked the deep, self-sacrificing love of a true mother.

The very different reactions of the two women are also conveyed in the use of a jussive preceded by אַל to express a "temporary prohibition"[2] versus an imperfect preceded by לֹא to indicate a "permanent prohibition." The difference in nuance between these prohibitions is difficult to portray in English. The true mother's statement includes a "temporary prohibition" in the phrase אַל־תְּמִיתֻהוּ, "surely do not kill the child *now*." By contrast, the other woman betrays her utter disregard for the child's life when she makes use of a permanent prohibition in her declaration, "then he will *never* be to me or to you, divide (him)" (גַּם־לִי גַם־לָךְ לֹא יִהְיֶה גְּזֹרוּ). In essence she states, "If I cannot have the child, then no one will ever have him—go ahead and kill him."

This portrayal of the self-sacrificing love of one human

mother is a glimpse of the infinitely greater love of our heavenly Father, who was willing to give up his own Son so that we might live forever in his presence.

Paul D. Wegner

Notes

1. Mike Butterworth, רחם, *NIDOTTE*, 3:1093

2. See GKC, §§ 107o–p; 109c–f; Williams, §§396, 402; Waltke and O'Connor, 34n6; etc. Paul Joüon is one of the few who seems uncertain of this structure (*Grammaire de L'hébreu biblique*, 2nd ed. [Rome: Pontifical Biblical Institute, 1996], 310 §114i).

Turned Like a Little Child

2 KINGS 5:14

MT	NASB
וַיֵּרֶד וַיִּטְבֹּל בַּיַּרְדֵּן שֶׁבַע פְּעָמִים	So he went down and dipped *himself* seven times in the Jordan,
כִּדְבַר אִישׁ הָאֱלֹהִים	according to the word of the man of God;
וַיָּשָׁב בְּשָׂרוֹ כִּבְשַׂר נַעַר קָטֹן	and his flesh was restored like the flesh of a little child
וַיִּטְהָר:	and he was clean.

You probably know the story. Naaman, a powerful Syrian general, was a leper. A captive slave girl mentioned that a prophet dwelt in Israel who could cure him. Naaman traveled there, and Elisha told him to dip himself in the Jordan seven times. He grumbled at this, thinking it was beneath his dignity, but in the end he did it — and he emerged healed! Note the verb ירד ("to go down, dip") and its similarity to the name "Jordan," יַרְדֵּן. Most likely this is a wordplay (found elsewhere in the Hebrew Bible; e.g., Josh 3:13; 1 Kgs 2:8).

The beginning of the story emphasizes Naaman's importance and power, and the little maid (נַעֲרָה קְטַנָּה) is his polar opposite: no status, no office, no prominence (5:2). What a change then, when Naaman emerged from the Jordan the seventh time, with skin "like a נַעַר קָטֹן"— the same description (with masculine gender) as the little maid. The thought is, he became like her. On the surface this refers to his skin, but there is a deeper meaning as well.

Note the use of the verb שׁוּב (glossed "restored"). It is repeated in the next verse (v. 15): Naaman "returned" or "turned" to the man of God to confess that there is no god but Israel's God. More than a change of skin has taken place. Naaman has become like the little maid in his faith as well. Sometimes this word is used for repentance, the turning of hearts; see 1 Kgs 8:48, "if they repent with all their mind and with all their heart . . ." (ESV). That's the idea. When Naaman emerged as it were from a baptism (in fact, the Old Greek uses βαπτίζω for his dips), he emerged a new man. He even took a plot of dirt from Israel home with him, promised to worship no god but the God of Israel, and confessed his disdain for Rimmon, the god of Syria.

The Old Greek uses στρέφω to translate שׁוּב in Naaman's story. This word is used in Matthew 18:2–4 (ESV), "And calling to him a child, he put him in the midst of them and said, 'Truly, I say to you, unless you turn [στρέφω] and become like children, you will never enter the kingdom of heaven. Whoever humbles himself like this child is the greatest in the kingdom of heaven.'" To be great in the kingdom, Christians must *turn* and be like a little child. Naaman's attitude toward Elisha in the end is what our attitude must be toward Christ—humble, grateful, singular trust, like the little maid.

Naaman the leper emerged "clean." Uncleanness is contagious; whoever touched a leper became unclean. But when Jesus touched lepers, his cleanness made the leper clean (see Matt 8:3). Jesus actually cited Naaman's case as being paradigmatic for his earthly ministry (Luke 4:27). His ministry is to cleanse outsiders, bringing them into the kingdom. Every Gentile Christian is part of that work; Jesus brings in those who were outside.

Someday, like Naaman, our flesh also will be made new, and we will shine forth in glory (1 Cor 15:41 – 52). Amen, come Lord Jesus!

George Schwab

So Near, Yet So Far

ISAIAH 5:7

MT	NIV
כִּי כֶרֶם יְהוָה צְבָאוֹת	The vineyard of the LORD Almighty
בֵּית יִשְׂרָאֵל	is the nation of Israel,
וְאִישׁ יְהוּדָה	and the people of Judah
נְטַע שַׁעֲשׁוּעָיו	are the vines he delighted in.
וַיְקַו לְמִשְׁפָּט	And he looked for justice,
וְהִנֵּה מִשְׂפָּח	but saw bloodshed;
לִצְדָקָה	for righteousness,
וְהִנֵּה צְעָקָה:	but heard cries of distress.

In Isaiah 5, the prophet Isaiah sings a song "for the one I love" about a vineyard, perhaps at a harvest festival. The song starts off with what appears to be a delightful love song. It soon becomes clear, however, that this is not Isaiah's song but Yahweh's song. Isaiah uses this song to express God's disappointment that his people are not bringing forth the fruit in their individual lives and in the life of the nation that he, their vinedresser, should have expected.

Yahweh had freely tended his vineyard with every possible bit of love and care (5:1 – 2a). Thus, he had anticipated a luscious, plump, juicy crop of grapes at the time of harvest. Instead, "it yielded only bad fruit" (5:2b). In 5:3 – 4 Yahweh then asks the nation what else he could have done to pamper his vineyard; he had used all of the latest techniques to guarantee a great harvest. So Isaiah follows up in 5:5–6 with harsh words of judgment. Then, as Isaiah closes this song in v. 7, he uses a powerful wordplay that summarizes well Yahweh's feelings about what has been happening to his people. Wordplays occur in every language; poets (and Isaiah is a poet) are particularly adept at expressing profound thoughts in as few words as possible. Such wordplays greatly enrich our understanding of the power of God's message.[1]

In v. 7, just in case God's people have not caught on about the true referent for the vineyard, the prophet formally identifies the vineyard as "the nation of Israel ... the people of Judah" (5:7a). Then, in 5:7b he offers his clever, yet heart-rending wordplay: "And he looked for justice (מִשְׁפָּט) but saw bloodshed (מִשְׂפָּח); for righteousness (צְדָקָה), but heard cries of distress (צְעָקָה)." In transliterated Hebrew, Yahweh looked for *mišpāṭ* from his people and got *miśpāḥ* instead; he looked for *ṣĕdāqâ* and got *ṣĕʿāqâ* instead.

Here were God's people—so close to what he expected, and yet so far away. Note how there are only a couple of sounds different between these two pairs of words, and yet in terms of their meaning, they are miles apart—justice versus bloodshed, righteous living versus distressful wails. Put otherwise, from Isaiah 1:10–15 we know that the Israelites were doing all the right rituals as prescribed in God's law, but when you looked beneath the veneer, they were out to serve themselves rather than Yahweh their God and his will for them.

But isn't that sometimes like us? We can do all the things that outwardly look good, at least as far as other people are concerned, but if our hearts are not in the things we do, we are miles away from what God wants us to be and become. God does not want a surface Christianity; rather, he wants a heartfelt love relationship with him. Isaiah powerfully gets that message across through the words he uses.

Verlyn D. Verbrugge

Notes

1. Note, for example, the wordplays on the names of the sons of Jacob in Genesis 29:31 – 30:13 or the town names mentioned in Micah 1:8 – 16; both of these sets are pointed out in the NIV footnotes.

The Silent Question and Answer

MT	NIV
מַשָּׂא דּוּמָה	[11] An oracle concerning Dumah:
אֵלַי קֹרֵא מִשֵּׂעִיר	Someone calls to me from Seir,
שֹׁמֵר מַה־מִלַּיְלָה	"Watchman, what is left of the night?
שֹׁמֵר מַה־מִלֵּיל:	Watchman, what is left of the night?"
אָמַר שֹׁמֵר	[12] The watchman replies,
אָתָה בֹקֶר וְגַם־לָיְלָה	"Morning is coming, but also the night.
אִם־תִּבְעָיוּן בְּעָיוּ	If you would ask, then ask;
שֻׁבוּ אֵתָיוּ:	and come back yet again."

Appropriating the biblical concept of the role of a "lookout" to the contemporary ecclesiastical context is an intriguing area of reflection. In the context of the oracles against foreign nations (21:1 – 17), the subdued Isaianic emotions embedded in the seeming silent question and answer in Isaiah 21:11 – 12 provides a window to look into the mind of the watchman/watchwoman. Besides watchfulness, diligence and perseverance

(21:6–9), what is required of Isaiah is the engagement of his whole being (21:11–12).

Isaiah 21:11–12 is a "silent" question and answer because these verses represent an imaginary dialogue going on within the mind of Isaiah. And Dumah, דּוּמָה, also means "silence" from the Hebrew root דמם. Thus, the prophet imagines someone calling to him from Seir and addressing him as the "watchman."

It is within this silent dialogue that two hidden but important emotive dimensions are evident. First, in replying to the query from Seir, the prophet refers to himself in the third person, ("The watchman replies...," v. 12). Thus, there exists a distance and objectiveness to whatever message is conveyed. Second and more elaborately, it is structured with a subtle, yet emphatic question ("Watchman, what is left of the night?" repeated twice in v. 11) with an equally subtle yet emphatic answer in v. 12. The question — "What is left of the night?" — is asked twice, and both times Isaiah is addressed as "Watchman." The repetition points to the questioner's sense of indeterminability/uncertainty of the night, the feeling of anxious waiting. It also implies that it is the watchman's duty to attend to such an inquiry, to be on guard through the night until morning comes.

In attending to the inquiry, Isaiah replies, "Morning is coming but also the night." Against the background of the feelings associated with the watchman's duties (impatience, v. 8; anxiety over the endless wait, v. 9; and the constant demand for diligence and perseverance, vv. 7–9), one finds here a direct reference to a hidden emotion — a deep sigh over the fact that the dawn will certainly come, but before it arrives, there will still be a long, uncertain period of darkness. The second part of the answer (v. 12b) ends emphatically with three imperatives: inquire! (בְּעָיוּ), return! (שֻׁבוּ), come! (אֵתָיוּ); "If you earnestly inquire, inquire! Return! Come!" Apparently, this answer gives no specific reply and is puzzling to many. However, when it is cast in the context of an anxious and earnest quest for knowing as implied in the question, then it means a lot to those who ask. In other words, when Isaiah is asked what is going to happen in the night before morning finally comes, he replies: "I don't really know, but don't give up. I invite you to keep asking." A two-fold affirmation is given: first, morning will certainly come, though we are still in the night. Second, keep returning to God/the watchman in your quest for understanding.

This prophecy against Dumah is short and enigmatic. Understood as the imaginary of a silent question and answer, it betrays a state of subtle but deep emotion. Lacking for answers, Isaiah is frustrated and helpless. Yet in the second portion of his response— inquire! (בְּעָיוּ), return! (שֻׁבוּ), come! (אֵתָיוּ)— he finds resolve. It is only in such inner dialogue can space be created to resolve such tensions. Isaiah 21:11–12, then, provides us an example of the prophet's inner world as he seeks to fulfill his role as God's appointed watchman.

Barbara M. Leung Lai

Taking a Conjunction Seriously ... Twice

MT	ESV
וְלָכֵן יְחַכֶּה יְהוָה לַחֲנַנְכֶם	[a] Therefore the LORD waits to be gracious to you,
וְלָכֵן יָרוּם לְרַחֶמְכֶם	[b] and therefore he exalts himself to show mercy to you.
כִּי־אֱלֹהֵי מִשְׁפָּט יְהוָה	[c] For the LORD is a God of justice;
אַשְׁרֵי כָּל־חוֹכֵי לוֹ:	[d] blessed are all those who wait for him.

Isaiah 30:18 seems jarring in its context. Judah has been stubbornly rebellious, and judgment is about to fall (30:1–17). Suddenly v. 18 describes Yahweh as "waiting" (חכה) to be gracious, and the rest of the chapter describes how Yahweh will bless Judah. Although prophetic books contain other abrupt switches from judgment to mercy (e.g., Hos 1:9 vs. 2:1), Isaiah 30:18 seems to contradict v. 17 rather than simply giving a picture of a grace-filled future. As Wildberger puts it, "After the announcements of judgment in 30:1–17, Isaiah could never have said that Yahweh was still playing a waiting game with the judgment, because he wanted to offer mercy."[1] This apparent incongruity is sharpened by the fact that v. 18 begins with וְלָכֵן ("and therefore").

Instead of following Wildberger, however, in positing contradictory oracles by multiple authors stitched together by a non sequitur וְלָכֵן, we should take וְלָכֵן seriously and reexamine the logical flow of Isaiah 30. Assyria threatened Judah, so without consulting Yahweh, Judah asked Egypt to protect them militarily (vv. 1–7). Yahweh denounced this through his prophets (vv. 1–7), but the people rejected his message (vv. 8–12) and continued to rely on diplomatic stratagems (vv. 12, 15). As a result, Yahweh promises that their strategy of appealing to Egypt will be destroyed (vv. 12–14), and they will be defeated militarily (vv. 16–17). Nevertheless, this is not the end. As soon as his people call out to him, Yahweh will be gracious to them and answer them (v. 19). He will afflict them (v. 20) and make them hear his direction (vv. 20–21). As a result, they will repent (v. 22), and he will bless them agriculturally (vv. 23–25), heal their wounds (v. 26), and defeat Assyria to the joy of his people (vv. 27–33).

Within this context, 30:18 is the hinge. The conjunction וְלָכֵן indicates that this verse is a result of vv. 1–17, not a contradiction to it. It is not that Yahweh is delaying judgment in order to be gracious; that would contradict vv. 1–17. Instead, he is going to judge, and therefore (וְלָכֵן, v. 18a) he is delaying grace (vv. 19–33). Judah has put their hope in Egypt instead of waiting on Yahweh (חוֹכֵי לֹו, v. 18d; cf. v. 15). Therefore (וְלָכֵן, v. 18a) his grace (חנן, v. 18a) will also wait (חכה, v. 18a) while he judges them (vv. 1–17).

Why does Yahweh delay grace while Judah calls on Egypt? The repeated conjunction וְלָכֵן in v. 18b indicates the answer. As a result (וְלָכֵן) of delaying grace (v. 18a), when Yahweh does have mercy (רחם, v. 18b), it exalts him (רום). Because (כִּי, v. 18c) Yahweh is a God of justice, he delivers those who rely on him (v. 18d). If Yahweh were to deliver Judah while they relied on Egypt, that would exalt Egypt. But if he delivers Judah when they rely on him, that exalts him. Yahweh exalts himself by making his grace wait until people wait on him.

As long as we lack faith, calling on Egypt to deliver us (like Judah), we can expect the grace of the God of justice to wait. Instead, when Assyria threatens us, let's wait on Yahweh, calling on him to deliver us, and let's bank everything on Isaiah's promise that "blessed are all those who wait for him."

John C. Beckman

Notes

1. Hans Wildberger, *Isaiah 28–39*, trans. T. H. Trapp (Minneapolis: Fortress, 2002), 170–71.

The Suffering Servant

MT	NIV
נִבְזֶה וַחֲדַל אִישִׁים אִישׁ מַכְאֹבוֹת וִידוּעַ חֹלִי	3 He was despised and rejected by mankind, a man of suffering, and familiar with pain.
וּכְמַסְתֵּר פָּנִים מִמֶּנּוּ נִבְזֶה וְלֹא חֲשַׁבְנֻהוּ׃	Like one from whom people hide their faces he was despised, and we held him in low esteem.
אָכֵן חֳלָיֵנוּ הוּא נָשָׂא וּמַכְאֹבֵינוּ סְבָלָם	4 Surely he took up our pain and bore our suffering,
וַאֲנַחְנוּ חֲשַׁבְנֻהוּ נָגוּעַ	yet we considered him punished by God,
מֻכֵּה אֱלֹהִים וּמְעֻנֶּה׃	stricken by him, and afflicted.
וְהוּא מְחֹלָל מִפְּשָׁעֵנוּ	5 But he was pierced for our transgressions,
מְדֻכָּא מֵעֲוֺנֹתֵינוּ	he was crushed for our iniquities;
מוּסַר שְׁלוֹמֵנוּ עָלָיו וּבַחֲבֻרָתוֹ נִרְפָּא־לָנוּ׃	the punishment that brought us peace was on him, and by his wounds we are healed.

This passage from Isaiah provides a haunting description of the Servant of the Lord, who humbly saves his people through pain and suffering. The people, however, seem to have no concern for him, nor do they have any understanding of what he has done for them.

The selected verses employ two sets of wordplays that highlight the substitutionary nature of the servant's affliction. The first wordplay begins in v. 3, where the servant is described as being familiar with חֳלִי, "pain."[1] In the next verse, the servant actually takes, or carries, the חֳלִי of the people. The wordplay is carried further in v. 5 where the servant is described as being מְחֹלָל (mĕḥōlāl), which sounds very much like חֳלִי (ḥōlî). Most translations render this word as "pierced," which is a valid option, given the parallelism with מְדֻכָּא, "crushed," in the next line. However, the root חלל has a more common homonym, usually translated "polluted, defiled," which should also be considered, given the wider context of sickness and sin in this poem.[2] In either case, the servant takes the sickness of the people, associated with their sin, so that they can be well and whole (שָׁלוֹם).

The second wordplay focuses on the word מַכְאֹב, "pain, suffering." In v. 3 the poem describes the servant as being a man of מַכְאֹב. As in the previous wordplay, the next verse uses the same word to describe what the servant carries for the people. The servant takes on precisely what has been causing the people misery. Again, however, v. 5 takes the second wordplay just a little further. In this case, the servant not only carries the מַכְאֹב (mak'ōb) of the people, but he is also "crushed," מְדֻכָּא (mĕdukkā') for them, for their sin. One can hear the sound correspondence between the two words מַכְאֹב and מְדֻכָּא and follow the logical flow of the poem to find that the servant has gone above and beyond what is expected to save his people and restore them to health: "The punishment that brought us peace was on him, and by his wounds we are healed" (53:5).

The Suffering Servant is no stranger to us. Our Lord and

Savior Jesus Christ came in human flesh to save and redeem us. Without fanfare, he exchanged our sickness for his health, our pain for his peace. What is more, he willingly went beyond this to meet our deepest need: forgiveness of sin, which is the root cause of our sickness and pain. He took the punishment we deserved in order to bring us health, wholeness, peace, and ultimately eternity in relationship with himself.

Jennifer E. Noonan

Notes

1. Other versions, including NIV (1984), translate חֹלִי as "suffering" in v. 3. However, this obscures the wordplay.

2. It is also plausible that the author included some intentional ambiguity here, wanting the audience to wrestle with both meanings of the word מְחֹלָל.

The Call of Jeremiah

JEREMIAH 1:5

MT	NIV
בְּטֶרֶם אֶצָּרְךָ בַבֶּטֶן יְדַעְתִּיךָ	Before I formed you in the womb I knew you,
וּבְטֶרֶם תֵּצֵא מֵרֶחֶם הִקְדַּשְׁתִּיךָ	before you were born I set you apart;
נָבִיא לַגּוֹיִם נְתַתִּיךָ׃	I appointed you as a prophet to the nations.

When we think about the phrase "God appoints," we tend to associate it with God's sovereign choice. God appears as an authority figure, putting a grave responsibility on some human being, such as Jeremiah, to fulfill his mission. However, in the Hebrew text the word translated "appoint" means, quite literally, "give" (נתן). God *gives* Jeremiah the role of a prophet to all nations. Being a prophet is not just a call, a responsibility, a mission, and a task. It is a gift from God.

In fact, the verb "give" (נתן) occurs three more times in Jeremiah 1 (vv. 9, 15, 18). In 1:5 God gives Jeremiah the office of the prophet. In 1:9 God gives Jeremiah his word. God stretched out his hands, touched Jeremiah's mouth, and said to him, "Behold, I have given [נתן, NIV 'put'] my words in your mouth." Jeremiah does not need to worry about what to say because God has given him his words. This is also God's gift.

In v. 15, God continues his words to Jeremiah. God said he would call all the families of the kingdoms of the north; they would come and "will set up [נתן] their thrones in the entrance of the gates of Jerusalem; they will come against all her surrounding walls and against all the towns of Judah." God forewarns Jeremiah what is to come. As God's instrument of judgment, nations from the north would come and "give" their reign at the gates of Jerusalem to overthrow it. This judgment is also "given" by God in the sense that this is under God's sovereign plan.

In 1:18 God concludes his commission to Jeremiah by saying, "Now, behold, I have given [נתן] you today as a fortified city, and as a pillar of iron and as walls of bronze against the whole land, to the kings of Judah, to its princes, to its priests, and to the people of the land." God even cares for Jeremiah's emotional state by giving him a spirit as tough as a fortified city in order to stand against all opposition. As Jeremiah's life and ministry turn out, he faces opposition from all sides, including people in his hometown, priests, kings, and the people of Judah. Emotional strength that can endure hardship and persevere against all odds is also a gift from God.

Being a prophet is a gift from God. When God gives Jeremiah the gift of a prophet, God also endows the gift of words and the gift of emotional strength to him. One cannot do God's work effectively without all three elements. Even external circumstances such as the enemy's opposition are allowed by God to accomplish his work. God is the source of all things. God gives!

We may want to examine our own attitude when we serve God. Do we see it as a gift from God or as a burden to carry? Do we use our own wisdom and words in accomplishing God's task, or do we use the gifts that God has granted to us? Can our emotions withstand the adversity coming our way? We need to trust that God has given us all we need in order to do his work!

Chloe Sun

Universal Guilt, Unlimited Grace

JEREMIAH 25:15, 26b

MT	NIV
כִּי כֹה אָמַר יְהוָה אֱלֹהֵי יִשְׂרָאֵל אֵלַי	[15] This is what the LORD, the God of Israel, said to me:
קַח אֶת־כּוֹס הַיַּיִן הַחֵמָה הַזֹּאת מִיָּדִי	"Take from my hand this cup filled with the wine of my wrath
וְהִשְׁקִיתָה אֹתוֹ אֶת־כָּל־הַגּוֹיִם	and make all the nations
אֲשֶׁר אָנֹכִי שֹׁלֵחַ אוֹתְךָ אֲלֵיהֶם:	to whom I send you drink it."
וּמֶלֶךְ שֵׁשַׁךְ יִשְׁתֶּה אַחֲרֵיהֶם:	[26b] And after all of them, the king of Sheshak will drink it too.

At this point in Judah's history, their faithlessness and disobedience to God had brought them to the brink of destruction. They had been repeatedly attacked by the Babylonians and would have welcomed divine intervention on their behalf, even if it was undeserved. How comforting, then, for the people of Judah to hear Jeremiah's prophecy against "all the nations" (כָּל־הַגּוֹיִם). Hidden at the end of the list was one nation they would agree it most: "the king of Sheshak." "Sheshak" (שֵׁשַׁךְ) is rendered in *atbash* writing, which represents the Hebrew letters of a word in reverse alphabetical order. So, for "Sheshak," *š*

(שׁ, the second letter from the end of the alphabet) represents *b* (בּ, the second letter from the beginning of the alphabet) and *k* (ך, the eleventh letter from the end of the alphabet) represents *l* (ל, the eleventh letter from the beginning of the alphabet). Thus, שׁשַׁך represents בבל, or בָּבֶל ("Babylon"). The people of Judah would be relieved to hear that the coming judgment would culminate in the judgment of Babylon, the archetypical enemy of God and his people.

What they would not have expected, however, was that they too would be on the divine hit list. In fact, they headed the list! When the people of Judah heard about God's coming judgment on the nations (v. 15), they no doubt thought it meant the *other* nations. How utterly shocking, then, to hear Jeremiah list "Jerusalem and the towns of Judah" among all the nations who would experience God's judgment (v. 18)!

Indeed, the coming divine judgment Jeremiah foresees will extend "to all the kingdoms on the face of the earth" (כָּל־הַמַּמְלְכוֹת הָאָרֶץ אֲשֶׁר עַל־פְּנֵי הָאֲדָמָה, 25:26). The judgment is described as a cup (כּוֹס; LXX: ποτήριον) filled with the wine of God's wrath that every person on earth would have to drink because all are guilty of sin and have fallen short of the glory of God (Rom 3:23).

Into this dark reality the light of God's grace will shine brightly when his own Son, the only guiltless human being who ever lived, offers to drink for all of us guilty ones this cup filled with the wine of God's wrath. This is the cup (ποτήριον) Jesus prayed would pass from him, if possible (Luke 22:42). Only he could fully comprehend the magnitude of God's wrath against every human sin. And yet, with incomprehensible grace, Jesus chose to pay that price. For all of us who put our faith in him, his experience of God's wrath is counted as our own. When we acknowledge that we, too, are among the guilty who deserve to drink the cup of God's wrath and put our faith in the one who graciously drank that cup for us, our new relationship with God (in Jeremiah's words, the "new covenant") that Jesus accomplishes for us is just as secure and unbreakable as Jesus' relationship with the Father. To use the words of the old hymn, God's "grace is greater than all our sin."

Michael J. Williams

God Feeds His Sheep with Justice

EZEKIEL 34:16

MT	NIV
אֶת־הָאֹבֶדֶת אֲבַקֵּשׁ	I will search for the lost
וְאֶת־הַנִּדַּחַת אָשִׁיב	and bring back the strays.
וְלַנִּשְׁבֶּרֶת אֶחֱבֹשׁ	I will bind up the injured
וְאֶת־הַחוֹלָה אֲחַזֵּק	and strengthen the weak,
וְאֶת־הַשְּׁמֵנָה וְאֶת־הַחֲזָקָה אַשְׁמִיד	but the sleek and the strong I will destroy.
אֶרְעֶנָּה בְמִשְׁפָּט׃	I will shepherd the flock with justice.

Ezekiel 34:16 comes after God's indictment against the shepherds, Israel's leaders, who have not been taking care of God's sheep, his people Israel. In vv. 10–11, due to the shepherds' mistreatment of the sheep, Yahweh states that he will shepherd the sheep himself.

In vv. 12–15 Yahweh states how he will care for his sheep in all the ways that the shepherds did not. In line with this, v. 16 echoes and inverts vv. 3–4. After describing his actions to help the sheep, the final phrase in v. 16 states: אֶרְעֶנָּה בְמִשְׁפָּט, translated, "I will shepherd the flock with justice" (NIV). But because of ambiguity in the verb and the noun, this phrase has been translated in different ways. First, the verb רעה is translated "shepherd" in NIV and HCSB, "tend" in CEB, and "feed" in NRSV, KJV, ESV, and NASB. When considered in the context of sheep, this range of meanings is common. But when referring to people, this verb would more appropriately be translated "rule." With this meaning in mind, this verse describes the character of God's rule as king. God's rule over the people will be just, "I will rule them with justice." This multivalence would likely not be lost on readers thinking of God as a shepherd who is king, a common title for rulers in the ancient Near East.[1]

A second ambiguity in this final phrase is whether the noun מִשְׁפָּט (justice, judgment) is only a negative "judgment" describing the final phrase of the verse where God judges the strong or whether it is a summative statement of "justice" and potentially includes both the positive and negative aspects of his justice (caring for the poor while giving negative judgment to the strong). The echo of vv. 3–4 makes it more likely that the phrase is summative. In v. 4 the description of the bad shepherds ruling the sheep harshly summarizes all of their actions in vv. 2–3; similarly in v. 16, Yahweh's ruling with justice summarizes all of his actions in vv. 11–16.

Another aspect of the Hebrew language often lost in translation is the structuring of the object to verb relationship, which creates the echo with vv. 3–4. In vv. 3–4 and in v. 16, the object is placed at the front of the sentence. The purpose of fronting the object may be to create focus on the objects—the weak, the sick, the injured, the lost—who deserve to be remembered. They were forgotten by their leaders, but God himself will remember and care for them.

The point is twofold for us. First, we, like the shepherds, are indicted if we forget these needy ones in our midst, for not only are the leaders critiqued for their actions, but the sheep are too (vv. 17–19). Whom have we forgotten or trampled on in our desire for getting good things for ourselves?

Second, we see God's character of love for the weakest and hurting among us. He is the true leader and the true shepherd. Jesus will later use Ezekiel 34 to describe himself in John 10 in the famous Good Shepherd discourse. This is the continuing character of our God to feed his people with justice, to rule his kingdom with מִשְׁפָּט (justice).

Beth M. Stovell

Notes

1. See Beth M. Stovell, "Yahweh as Shepherd-King in Ezekiel 34: Linguistic-Literary Analysis of Metaphors of Shepherding," in *Modeling Biblical Language: Papers from the McMaster Divinity College Linguistics Circle*, eds. Stanley E. Porter, Wally F. Cirafesi, and Greg Fewster; Linguistic Biblical Studies (Leiden: Brill, forthcoming).

I Am Not I Am

MT	NRSV
וַיֹּאמֶר קְרָא שְׁמוֹ לֹא עַמִּי	Then the LORD said, "Name him Lo-ammi,
כִּי אַתֶּם לֹא עַמִּי	for you are not my people
וְאָנֹכִי לֹא־אֶהְיֶה לָכֶם׃	and I am not your God."

Honey. Sweetie. Dear. Beloved. Spouses often choose different pet names for each other. Similarly, parents and children possess a vocabulary unique and exclusive to the family: Mommy. Daddy. Sweetie. Darling. Naming within the bounds of marriage and family carries special significance today — and back in the days of the Old Testament. Names in the Bible are not mere arbitrarily determined signifiers of the signified in the semiotic model of de Saussure.[1] Instead, names often possess a correlation to the person who is identified by the name. In addition, the act of naming bears great significance, for it often signifies the establishment of a new relationship between the person named and the person granting the name.

Naming of family members plays a prominent role in Hosea 1. In v. 4 Hosea is commanded to name his first son Jezreel (יִזְרְעֶאל), which means "he sows"; in v. 6 the prophet names his daughter Lo-ruhamah (לֹא רֻחָמָה), which means "no compassion"; and in v. 9 God commands Hosea to name his last son Lo-ammi (לֹא עַמִּי) ("not my people"). While certainly God's lack of compassion and disavowal of peoplehood would trouble Israel, these names are all the more alarming because they are covenantal terms. God's words in Exodus 6:7, "I will take you as my people (עַם), and I will be your God" (NRSV), follow a pattern of covenant formulaic speech[2] that carries a performative function. In a manner similar to that of a man and a woman sealing a marriage with the vows, "I *do*," God seals a covenant relationship with Israel with these words. Thus God's speech in Hosea 1:9, "for you are not my people and I am not your God," can be understood as a reversal of the covenant formula of Exodus 6:7. It is analogous to one betrothed saying to another at the wedding ceremony, "I *don't*."

This understanding of Hosea 1:9 can be gleaned from English versions, but when examined in the Hebrew, another meaning surfaces. The words "your God" do not appear in the Hebrew. The Hebrew literally reads, "For you are not my people and I am not your *I am*." In fact, these two phrases are set in a parallel relationship in the Hebrew such that "not my people" mirrors "not your I am." "I am" (אֶהְיֶה) is God's self-designated description in Exodus 3:14, "I am who I am" (אֶהְיֶה אֲשֶׁר אֶהְיֶה). The word אֶהְיֶה is the *qal* imperfect 1cs form of the verb היה ("to be") and appears to be a wordplay on the name of God יהוה, known as the Tetragrammaton (YHWH). יהוה can be construed as the *qal* or *hiphil* imperfect 3ms form of the verb היה/ הוה. Regardless of its etymology, יהוה is God's eternal name and the covenant name between God and his people Israel (Exod 3:15; 6:1 – 8). "I am" can be viewed as a description or even a nickname for God, used only by insiders within his family. In this case, the Hebrew makes clear that Hosea 1:9 does not only nullify covenant vows, but it eviscerates God's covenant name from Israel's vocabulary.

I cannot imagine what it would be like should my children be taken from my custody and could no longer call me "Dad." I cannot imagine what it would be like should my marriage end and my wife no longer refer to me as her husband. The sad message of Hosea is that Israel is cut off from God's covenant. God will no longer call them "my people," and they can no longer call God YHWH or describe him as "I am." Yet the good news of Hosea is that a future day is coming when God will restore his people such that he "will say to Lo-ammi, 'You are my people'; and he shall say, 'You are my God'" (Hos 2:23 [25], NRSV). Thanks be to God that through Jesus Christ we can be called "my people" (cf. Rom 9:25–26), and we can worship the great "I am," YHWH (cf. Rev 1:8).

Bo H. Lim

Notes

1. Ferdinand de Saussure, *Course in General Linguistics*, eds. Charles Bally and Albert Sechehaye; trans. Wade Baskin (New York: McGraw-Hill, 1966), 67–78.

2. Rolf Rendtorff, *The Covenant Formula: An Exegetical and Theological Investigation*, trans. M. Kohl; OTS (Edinburgh: T&T Clark, 1998), 13.

Who Knows? Those Who Repent!

JOEL 2:13b–14a

MT	NIV
וְשׁוּבוּ אֶל־יְהוָה אֱלֹהֵיכֶם	[13b] Return to the LORD your God,
כִּי־חַנּוּן וְרַחוּם הוּא	for he is gracious and compassionate,
אֶרֶךְ אַפַּיִם וְרַב־חֶסֶד	slow to anger and abounding in love,
וְנִחָם עַל־הָרָעָה:	and he relents from sending calamity.
מִי יוֹדֵעַ	[14a] Who knows?
יָשׁוּב וְנִחָם	He may turn and relent
וְהִשְׁאִיר אַחֲרָיו בְּרָכָה	and leave behind a blessing.

With these words, the prophet Joel invites God's people to repent. The invitation is given in the midst of God's judgment, after it has already been set in motion and there no longer seems to be any hope left. Indeed, God's judgment is described as an invasion of locusts that ravages the land and leaves nothing behind except a devastated and parched land that can no longer produce any food for man or beast. Can it get any worse than that?

What is not immediately obvious in the English text is that

these two verses echo two verses in the book of Jonah. Realizing that may change the way we understand Joel's invitation to repentance.

Like Joel, Jonah predicted total devastation, but unlike Joel, not on God's people, but on the enemy of God's people: the city of Nineveh. Like Joel, he too knew that God is a "gracious and compassionate God, slow to anger and abounding in love, a God who relents from sending calamity" (4:2). Jonah, like Joel, reverses "compassionate" and "gracious" from its order in Exodus 34:6, and like Joel, concludes that 34:6 implies that God "relents from sending calamity."

Joel's follow-up question, "Who knows? He may turn and relent" (2:14), is also found in Jonah. In decreeing a fast for the Ninevites, the king of Nineveh asked, "Who knows? He may turn and relent *and with compassion turn from his fierce anger so that we will not perish*" (emphasis added, Jonah 3:9). The Hebrew for "Who knows? He may turn and relent" in Joel 2:14 is word for word the same as "Who knows? God may yet relent" in Jonah 3:9. Thus, when Joel calls God's people to repent, adding the question "Who knows? He may turn and relent...," he may be hoping that his hearers/readers will, in their minds, complete the sentence with "*and with compassion...*," just as when someone begins quoting "For God so loved the world..." those who have memorized John 3:16 cannot but automatically finish the sentence in their minds with "... that he gave his one and only Son," even if the speaker does not. And if Joel's hearers/readers did so, the question "Who knows?" shifts from being one to which the answer is uncertain (as it was for the king of Nineveh) to a rhetorical, if not ironic, one, to which the answer is a loud, resounding, "We know that he will!" For the book of Jonah would have taught them that even when a pagan people whose condemnation has already been decreed repents, God turns and relents. If that is how God deals with the pagan enemies of his own people, how much more would he not do so for his *own* people if they repent?

By recognizing the textual similarities between Joel's invitation to repentance and the book of Jonah, Joel's message shifts from being one of wishful thinking—hopefully God will turn and relent—to one of certainty and comfort: we know that if we repent, God *will* turn and relent. By understanding Joel in light of Jonah, we have the assurance that no particular sin, regardless of how horrible it may be, nor even the sum total of our sins, no matter how numerous these may be, are ever beyond God's grace and compassion. If one truly repents, God *will* "turn and relent, and leave behind a blessing."

Brian Schultz

Sacrificing to Sin

AMOS 4:4–5

MT	ESV
בֹּאוּ בֵית־אֵל וּפִשְׁעוּ	[4a] "Come to Bethel, and transgress;
הַגִּלְגָּל הַרְבּוּ לִפְשֹׁעַ	[b] to Gilgal, and multiply transgression;
וְהָבִיאוּ לַבֹּקֶר זִבְחֵיכֶם	[c] bring your sacrifices every morning,
לִשְׁלֹשֶׁת יָמִים מַעְשְׂרֹתֵיכֶם:	[d] your tithes every three days;
וְקַטֵּר מֵחָמֵץ תּוֹדָה	[5a] offer a sacrifice of thanksgiving of that which is leavened,
וְקִרְאוּ נְדָבוֹת הַשְׁמִיעוּ	[b] and proclaim freewill offerings, publish them;
כִּי כֵן אֲהַבְתֶּם בְּנֵי יִשְׂרָאֵל	[c] for so you love to do, O people of Israel!"
נְאֻם אֲדֹנָי יְהוִה:	[d] declares the Lord GOD.

At first glance, Amos's call for worshipers to come to Bethel and Gilgal (key temple sites for the northern kingdom) to sin can be confusing. Because the bi-cola of lines 4ab and 4cd parallel syntactically through the "gapping" of their initial imperative verbs into their successive lines ("come" and "bring"), readers are led to evaluate how these two bi-cola may relate semantically.[1] Superficially, the bi-cola of 4ab and 4cd may seem antithetical in their contrast of transgression versus sacrifices and tithes. However, reading lines 4cd as semantically specifying lines 4ab (a form of synonymous parallelism) reveals that Israel sins *by means of* their sacrifices and tithes. Moreover, in line 5c, the כִּי causal clause explains that the people love to give offerings and tithes (the כֵן adverb refers anaphorically [backward] to the previous clauses of lines 4c–5b). Thus, the reader is faced with the puzzling question of how the people can be sinning through their love to offer sacrifices and offerings.

An inspection of the specific Hebrew terms for these sacrifices and offerings reveals that the eagerness to sacrifice and give offerings is rooted in their economic sins and desire to love themselves. In line 4c, "your sacrifices" (זִבְחֵיכֶם) are sacrifices of slain animals that were eaten by the worshiper. Thus, the call is for worshipers to come and enjoy their meats every morning — a luxury in the ancient Near East that may be lost on modern readers. In line 4d, "your tithes" (מַעְשְׂרֹתֵיכֶם) are those offerings that are to be a tenth of a person's income. However, these prosperous individuals who can afford to tithe and eat sacrificed meat so frequently are likely to be the same individuals whom Amos frequently indicts for their unjust economic gain (e.g., 2:8, 5:12, 8:4–6). In lines 5a–b, the call to bring the freewill offerings (נְדָבוֹת), a specific type of well-being offering (שֶׁלֶם), and thank offerings of leavened bread (מֵחָמֵץ תּוֹדָה) further indicts the people. These people mistake their unjustly gained economic prosperity for God's favor and eagerly thank God for their well-being (i.e., material abundance) because it also affords them the opportunity to publicize their seeming favor with God.

Amos exposes the hidden darkness of these seemingly good activities and good people. Because the sacrifices and offerings have been acquired through violence and injustice, they sin and blaspheme God by thanking him with that which comes at the expense of God's justice. Thus, the more they offer these sacrifices and offerings, the more they sin, and the more they indict themselves. With poetic flourish, Amos exposes the false exterior of the people's thankful state and judges them for their true nature of injustice, false pretense, and delusion.

Although today's church has no such offering or sacrificial system, Amos's lesson regarding our motives for thanksgiving, service, and tithing is relevant. We must constantly ask ourselves whether we are basking in God's glory or our own false glory, whether our tithes come from just sources or at the expense of God's widows and orphans, and whether we are truly loving God or ourselves.

Kevin Chau

Notes

1. In linguistic terminology, "gapping" is referred to as ellipsis. For more on this linguistic phenomena, see Cynthia L. Miller, "A Linguistic Approach to Ellipsis in Biblical Poetry," *BBR* 13, no. 2 (2003): 251–70.

The Kingship Belongs to YHWH!

OBADIAH 21

MT	NIV
וְעָלוּ מוֹשִׁעִים בְּהַר צִיּוֹן	Deliverers will go up on Mount Zion
לִשְׁפֹּט אֶת־הַר עֵשָׂו	to govern the mountains of Esau.
וְהָיְתָה לַיהוָה הַמְּלוּכָה׃	And the kingdom will be the LORD's.

We know little of the prophet Obadiah. Indeed, all that we know we learn from the little tractate he has left. This short book provides (1) his name, which means "servant of YHWH," (2) the nature of his prophetic experience, "vision," which reflects his supernatural insight into the workings of God, and (3) his message, a 291-word utterance that offers a remarkable window into his times.

Although the prophecy of Obadiah is usually set out as poetry in our Bibles, this depends on a loose definition of poetry. This transcript of his message to the people of Jerusalem in the wake of the city's destruction at the hands of the Babylonians is composed in a style that is rhetorically emphatic and transparently passionate. But these are not his private ruminations on his people's troubles. Rather, this utterance has its roots in divine revelation; YHWH has given him insight not only into Judah's future but also into the providential workings of God himself.

Judah's painful experiences in the early sixth century are almost unimaginable. Over an eleven-year period, survivors witnessed successively the Babylonian invasion, the deportation of the upper classes, the razing of Jerusalem and the temple, the slaughter of the population, and the scattering of the survivors. Meanwhile the Edomites, descendants of Esau and distant cousins of the Israelites, also abandoned them. Instead of standing up for their "brother," they had participated in the crimes against Jerusalem and Judah and clapped enthusiastically as the nation was being destroyed.

The intensity of this personal trauma was surpassed only by the people's theological turmoil. To those who were compromised in their theology, this tragedy proved either that YHWH was impotent in the face of the Babylonian god Marduk, or that he had betrayed his covenant and abandoned his people in their hour of need. In either case, it left many of the survivors spiritually paralyzed and emotionally devastated. Other prophets had warned Judah that this fate was the consequence of rebellion against YHWH, and that events would transpire precisely as YHWH had specified in the covenant (Lev 26; Deut 28), but the people had stubbornly resisted such pleas for repentance and spiritual renewal. Instead, they shook their fists in YHWH's face, infuriated by his betrayal.

What do you say to a people who are convinced their God has either died (cf. Ezek 8:14), or that he has failed to keep his covenant promises? "The kingship belongs to YHWH!" (וְהָיְתָה לַיהוָה הַמְּלוּכָה, Obad 21). He is not merely a petty king over a miniature fiefdom centered in Jerusalem; he is king of the cosmos. This theme carries through into the New Testament, where Jesus — YHWH incarnate — is declared to be sovereign over all. With superlative titles, 1 Timothy 6:14 – 15 declares Jesus to be "our Lord Jesus Christ ... the blessed and only Ruler, the King of kings and Lord of lords." The portrayal of Jesus as king over all climaxes in Revelation in the doxologies of his worshipers from the entire cosmos (Rev 5:12 – 13).

Herein lies the key to the significance of the book of Obadiah for us. In Christ, not only the prophecy of Obadiah, but all of God's promises to Israel are fulfilled. In Christ, Gentile believers are grafted into the vine and made heirs of those promises (Rom 11:17 – 24). In Christ, the mighty are cast down and the humble are exalted. In Christ, God vanquishes those who oppose him and his people (Col 2:15). In Christ, citizens of the kingdom of darkness are ushered into the kingdom of light (Col 1:13). In Christ, those who, like Israel, deserve judgment for their rebellion are reconciled to God (2 Cor 5:19). The dominion belongs to YHWH, incarnate in Jesus Christ! To him be the glory and dominion for ever and ever. Amen!

Daniel I. Block

"I Fear Yahweh"

JONAH 1:5, 9, 16

MT	NIV
וַיִּירְא֣וּ הַמַּלָּחִ֗ים וַיִּזְעֲקוּ֮ אִ֣ישׁ אֶל־אֱלֹהָיו֒ וַיָּטִ֜לוּ אֶת־הַכֵּלִ֨ים אֲשֶׁ֤ר בָּאֳנִיָּה֙ אֶל־הַיָּ֔ם לְהָקֵ֖ל מֵעֲלֵיהֶ֑ם וְיוֹנָ֗ה יָרַד֙ אֶל־יַרְכְּתֵ֣י הַסְּפִינָ֔ה וַיִּשְׁכַּ֖ב וַיֵּרָדַֽם׃	⁵ All the sailors were afraid and each cried out to his own god. And they threw the cargo into the sea to lighten the ship. But Jonah had gone below deck, where he lay down and fell into a deep sleep.
וַיֹּ֥אמֶר אֲלֵיהֶ֖ם עִבְרִ֣י אָנֹ֑כִי וְאֶת־יְהוָ֞ה אֱלֹהֵ֤י הַשָּׁמַ֙יִם֙ אֲנִ֣י יָרֵ֔א אֲשֶׁר־עָשָׂ֥ה אֶת־הַיָּ֖ם וְאֶת־הַיַּבָּשָֽׁה׃	⁹ He answered, "I am a Hebrew and I worship the LORD, the God of heaven, who made the sea and the dry land."
וַיִּֽירְא֧וּ הָאֲנָשִׁ֛ים יִרְאָ֥ה גְדוֹלָ֖ה אֶת־יְהוָ֑ה וַיִּֽזְבְּחוּ־זֶ֙בַח֙ לַֽיהוָ֔ה וַֽיִּדְּר֖וּ נְדָרִֽים׃	¹⁶ At this the men greatly feared the LORD, and they offered a sacrifice to the LORD and made vows to him.

The story of Jonah is one of those classic stories that many readers know. Jonah has no interest in bringing the lost souls of the evil Assyrians in Nineveh to Yahweh. What is ironic is Jonah's unintended evangelism to the pagans on the ship.

Jonah 1 is written in a common Hebrew structure called a chiasm. Chiasms are written in parallel lines from the outside of the unit to its center. The center verse tends to hold a pivotal episode or point of the unit.[1] The parallel verses may be linked by similar vocabulary, phrases, ideas, or themes.

A Yahweh throws a great wind on the sea (v. 4)
  B The (pagan) sailors are afraid and call on their gods (v. 5a)
    C The sailors throw cargo into the sea to save themselves (v. 5b)
      D The sailors approached Jonah to save the ship (v. 6)
        E The sailors cast lots, how to save themselves (v. 7a)
          F The sailors learn Jonah is responsible (v. 7b)
            G Questions for Jonah (v. 8)
              H *Jonah identifies himself as one who fears Yahweh* (v. 9)
            G′ More questions for Jonah (v. 10a)
          F′ The sailors learn how Jonah was responsible (v. 10b)
        E′ The sailors ask Jonah how to save themselves (v. 11)
      D′ Jonah reports how to save themselves (v. 12)
    C′ The men row hard to save themselves (v. 13)
  B′ The (pagan) sailors call on Yahweh (v. 14)
A′ The sailors throw Jonah into the sea, the sea is calm, and they fear Yahweh (vv. 15–16)

This chiasm is framed by the great storm on the sea that opens the story and ends with Jonah being cast into the stormy sea to calm it. The chiasm moves in toward the center and back out again with the sailors' fear and salvation from the stormy seas. The key verse in this chapter, as illustrated in the center of the chiasm (H), is where Jonah identifies himself as one who fears Yahweh, "I am a Hebrew, and I fear the LORD God (v. 9)." The NIV translates the Hebrew word for "fear" here as "worship." This misses the significance of the use of "fear" throughout this chapter. The sailors looked to their own gods for salvation and cry out to them in their *fear* (v. 5), only to find salvation in the God of Jonah. Now they pray to him and *fear* Yahweh greatly, for he is the one who saved them from the storm (v. 16).

The sailors "fear" the storm, but Jonah "fears the LORD," the same Hebrew word. Ironically, the sailors' "fear" of the storm is replaced by their eventual "fear" of Yahweh. This is a shift from a fear that anticipates destruction and death to a "fear" that reveres the Creator. God uses our "fear" and acknowledgment of him even in our imperfections and stubbornness.

Sara Fudge

Notes

1. Jerome T. Walsh, *Style and Structure in Biblical Hebrew Narrative* (Collegeville, MN: Liturgical, 2001), 18–19.

A Prophetic Landscape

MT	ESV
כִּי אֲנוּשָׁה מַכּוֹתֶיהָ	For her wound is incurable,
כִּי־בָאָה עַד־יְהוּדָה	and it has come to Judah;
נָגַע עַד־שַׁעַר עַמִּי	it has reached to the gate of my people,
עַד־יְרוּשָׁלָ͏ִם:	to Jerusalem.

Yosemite National Park in California is arguably God's greatest masterpiece of creative glory. The combination of majestic mountains, soaring pines, thunderous waterfalls, and a variety of wildlife create breathtaking vistas. In a similar vein, Micah 1:8–16 majestically combines repetition, historical allusions, cohortatives, and sound and sense plays to appeal to God's people to turn from sin (before it is too late) and to return to his glorious presence.

The first two sections (vv. 8–9 and vv. 10–12) end with the word Jerusalem. Each verse in the third section (vv. 13–15) ends with the word Israel. The second section begins (v. 10) and the third ends (v. 15) with an allusion to David. "Tell it not in Gath" (v. 10) echoes 2 Samuel 1:20, where David laments the death of Saul and Jonathan. In v. 15 Adullam is the place to which David fled as a fugitive from Saul (1 Sam 22:1). In the final section (v. 16), Micah speaks directly to the citizens of Jerusalem, warning them that disaster, deportation, and death await.

The four first-person verbs in v. 8 are all cohortatives, show-ing Micah's resolve ("I will lament," "I will wail," "I will go," and "I will make [lamentation]"). In v. 10, using another first person verb, Micah reveals that he has rolled in the dust, show-ing his profound grief (see Josh 7:6; 1 Sam 4:12; 2 Sam 13:19; Job 16:15; Jer 6:26) over the moral malaise of his compatriots and the impending doom that will envelope the countryside of his youth.

The context suggests that "her wound is incurable" in v. 9 refers to the collapse of the northern kingdom, Israel, and its capital, Samaria. It is just a matter of time before her fate will be Jerusalem's. Verse 3 makes clear that Yahweh is now his people's enemy. He is responsible for their destruction, though Assyrians or Babylonians may receive the credit. If the reader removes the vowel points from the Hebrew for "her wound" (the third word of v. 9), one can see "the blow from the Lord" (see also the text critical apparatus in *BHS*).

When we think a pun is clever, we call it punny. When we wish we had never heard it, it is punishment. In Micah 1:10–15 the prophet offers a series of clever, but not very funny, sound and sense wordplays that threaten the well-being of the nation. The spiritually calloused in Micah's crowd would have been just as happy never having heard Micah's words.

The sound wordplays are based in two words sharing similar root letters. Micah uses five sound plays: in v. 10 Gath (*gat*) and tell (*taggîdû*); in v. 11 Zaanan (*ṣaʾănān*) and come out (*yāṣěʾāh*); in v. 13 Lachish (*lākîš*) and (to the) chariots (*lārekeš*); in v. 14 Aczib (*ʾakzîb*) and deception (*ʾakzāb*); and in v. 15 Mareshah (*mārēšāh*) and conqueror (*hayyōrēš*).

The sense wordplays are equally stunning. In Beth-le-aphrah ("house of dust"), Micah has rolled himself in the dust (v. 10b). The inhabitants of Shaphir ("beauty town") will go forth in nakedness and in shame (v. 11a). Beth-ezel ("the house next door") will not be a safe place for those seeking protection from the invasion (v. 11c). The inhabitants of Maroth ("bitter town") will wait for good ("something better") to come, but since Jerusalem is also in a fight for its life, it is unable to bring the anticipated help (v. 12). The rulers of Jerusalem will have to give tribute/a dowry ("parting gifts") and Moresheth-gath ("betrothed town"), Micah's hometown, to another.

Micah 1:8–16 is a literary *tour de force.* Using sublime literary strategies the prophet pleads with Judah to grieve her sin and return to God before it is too late.

Mark Mangano

How Will God's Judgment Pass over You?

MT		NIV
וּבְשֶׁטֶף עֹבֵר כָּלָה יַעֲשֶׂה מְקוֹמָהּ	1:8a	But with an overwhelming flood he will make an end of Nineveh.
כִּי עַל־מִי לֹא־עָבְרָה רָעָתְךָ תָּמִיד׃	3:19c	For who has not felt your endless cruelty?

These two verses share a word having the same Hebrew root, עבר, which has been translated in two different ways in the NIV for the sake of smooth English. The basic meaning of the root is "to pass over" or "to pass through." Because the word is used in a verse near the beginning of the book and also in the last verse of the book, it forms a sort of inclusio that communicates the basic content of the book: divine judgment on Nineveh, the capital of the dreaded empire of Assyria, would *pass through* or *overwhelm* them because their "endless cruelty" had *passed through* or *overwhelmed* everyone else. The judgment described in this prophecy is an example of the principle of *lex talionis*, or judgment corresponding to the crime (i.e., an eye for an eye).

That God's judgment should overwhelm Nineveh was not inevitable. God offers himself as a secure "refuge" (מָעוֹז, 1:7) for all who trust in him. Indeed, Nineveh had found that refuge earlier in their history when God spared them after they had responded appropriately to the ministry of Jonah. But they had forgotten that earlier time, and now their refusal to take refuge in God, their refusal to trust in him, had left them exposed to the "overwhelming flood" of his divine wrath.

In Exodus 12:23, the same root, עבר, is contrastively paralleled with its synonym, פסח, to communicate the justice and mercy of God that are the alternative possibilities for the "passing over" of his judgment. The verse begins with a description of Yahweh as he "passes through [the land] to strike the Egyptians" (וְעָבַר יְהוָה לִנְגֹּף אֶת־מִצְרַיִם). The verse then ends with a description of Yahweh's passing over, or exempting, the Israelites from that same judgment of death (וּפָסַח יְהוָה עַל־הַפֶּתַח וְלֹא יִתֵּן הַמַּשְׁחִית לָבֹא אֶל־בָּתֵּיכֶם לִנְגֹּף "and Yahweh will pass by the doorway and will not give to the destroying one [permission] to go into your houses to strike [you]").

The alternative possibilities communicated by "passing over" are also, and especially, manifested in the redemptive work of Jesus. He came to have God's judgment flow over him so that mercifully it would pass over everyone who does, in fact, take refuge in him by faith. There is therefore an alternative to facing the overwhelming flood of God's judgment ourselves. We can find a refuge from it by placing our faith in the one who experienced it for us.

All of us were at one time like the people of Nineveh — enemies of God and deserving his judgment. But now by our faith in Jesus Christ, we have entered into the refuge of his love. God's judgment now passes over us instead of overwhelming us. Let's do what we can, by his power, to let other people know that there is a divine refuge for them as well from the overwhelming flood of God's judgment.

Michael J. Williams

By Faith

HABAKKUK 2:4

MT	NIV
הִנֵּה עֻפְּלָה לֹא־יָשְׁרָה נַפְשׁוֹ בּוֹ	See, the enemy is puffed up; his desires are not upright—
וְצַדִּיק בֶּאֱמוּנָתוֹ יִחְיֶה׃	but the righteous person will live by his faithfulness—

Sometimes it seems that God lets the righteous suffer at the hands of the empowered wicked. They may well wonder how they can live under such circumstances. Habakkuk felt indignant because the righteous in Jerusalem were suffering at the hands of their wicked leaders. Having learned that God was going to send the Babylonians to punish them, Habakkuk then complains about the fairness of using such people to "swallow up those more righteous than themselves" (1:13). Yahweh responds that Babylon will not escape God's wrath either (2:2–5).

This is the context for our verse. The three-word statement about the righteous man in 2:4b stands in stark contrast to the surrounding description (vv. 4–5) of the character of the wicked. The righteous man will flourish (חיה may include security and morality).[1] Even in poetry, noting the Hebrew word order gives insight. The clause begins with וְצַדִּיק, a *waw* plus a noun, marking a dramatic interruption in the statement about the wicked. It also serves as the subject of the verb יִחְיֶה. The key word, though, is בֶּאֱמוּנָתוֹ in the center of the clause. It may modify either the preceding noun or the following verb.

If בֶּאֱמוּנָתוֹ modifies וְצַדִּיק, then the entire phrase is a single constituent followed by the verb. The meaning would be approximately, "the one who is righteous by his faith shall live." The prepositional phrase gives the means by which one is counted righteous, namely, by his faith. The righteous one, whom Habakkuk had painted as the victim (1:4, 13), God describes as having to wait on the fulfillment of the vision. This one is righteous by his faith in Yahweh to carry out his will against the wicked both from inside and outside the borders of Judah. It is this one who will live successfully.

The second way to take the prepositional phrase is as a verbal modifier. In this case בֶּאֱמוּנָתוֹ forms a unit separate from וְצַדִּיק and thus becomes a second constituent before the verb and in turn becomes the focus. The meaning might be expressed, "By his faith is how the righteous one shall live." The significance is that the righteous one will live, but the means by which he truly lives is a life of faith. Many English translations take it so, as in the NIV, "the righteous person will live by his faithfulness." However, since this is normal English, the emphasis on בֶּאֱמוּנָתוֹ is lost. Again, in Habakkuk this is a faith in Yahweh to carry out his will. But taken as an adverb, the emphasis is on *how* the person will live. He will live in a manner that is a consequence of his faith; he lives morally in contrast to the corrupt ways of the wicked. In other words, faith carries with it a moral result: the outcome of living by faith is a godly life.

Both of these options are valid. Perhaps Habakkuk meant both. Likewise, Paul possibly has both meanings in mind when he quotes Habakkuk 2:4 at the close of his introduction to Romans. In Romans 1 – 11 a man who is righteous by faith will truly live, the first option; in Romans 12 – 16 a righteous man lives out his moral life on the basis of his faith, the second option. Both are always true for God's people even (especially?) amidst the apparent prosperity of the wicked.

Lee M. Fields

Notes

1. Elmer B. Smick, חָיָה, *TWOT* 1:279 – 81.

MT	NET
יְהוָה אֱלֹהַיִךְ בְּקִרְבֵּךְ	[a] The LORD your God is in your midst;
גִּבּוֹר יוֹשִׁיעַ	[b] he is a warrior who can deliver.
יָשִׂישׂ עָלַיִךְ בְּשִׂמְחָה	[c] He takes great delight in you;
יַחֲרִישׁ בְּאַהֲבָתוֹ	[d] he renews you by his love;
יָגִיל עָלַיִךְ בְּרִנָּה׃	[e] he shouts for joy over you.

The book of Zephaniah begins with a threat, warning that the day of Yahweh will come as judgment. God will bring utter ruin to Judah as he wipes out the worship of Baal. On that day, he will punish and they will wail. God will go through Jerusalem with lamps searching out those who thought Yahweh would do nothing. It will be a day of wrath, trouble, distress, destruction, devastation, darkness, gloom, clouds, and thick darkness. There will be no deliverance; Zephaniah foretells that Yahweh will make a complete end (1:18).

The shift beginning ch. 2 barely breaks the gloom. The call to seek Yahweh suggests that the righteous will "perhaps" (אוּלַי,

2:3) be hidden on the day of Yahweh's anger. The assurance of judgment throughout the world continues into ch. 3.

But along with fury and anger, Yahweh will purify, removing the proud and leaving the humble (3:9–13). Finally, with their character changed, the people are called to rejoice, a tremendous shift in mood. Judgment is removed, the enemy is turned back, and Yahweh dwells with his people. (How like the gospel!)

Yet there is some danger in that the people will still be paralyzed by fear (3:16). We then come to the final passage of assurance, where Zephaniah assures the people that Yahweh will be with them (3:17a) as a delivering warrior (v. 17b). Yahweh, who was angry, now rejoices over them (v. 17c, e). But here the translations vary. What is it that Yahweh will do (v. 17d)? The KJV says "he will rest in his love," perhaps meaning rest from his wrath? The NIV (1984) says "he will quiet you with his love," perhaps like a mother quieting an anxious child? And NET says "he renews you by his love," a reference to restoration?

The MT attests the *hiphil* form of the stative root חרשׁ. The *hiphil* of a stative root often means to act in a manner characterized by the attribute in the stative verb. This would mean "he remains silent in his love" (hence the KJV and NASB). But this contradicts the shouts of joy in the surrounding lines.

Some propose a causative meaning, appealing to Job 11:3 as an example, "he will quiet you" (so the NIV). Again, shouts of joy would seem an odd way to quiet someone, but the appeal to Job is faulty. Job 11:3a seemingly may be read as "Will your idle talk reduce others to silence?" or as "Should men remain silent at your boasts." The following parallel line (asking if none should rebuke him) suggests the latter is correct. Thus for every other Hiphil occurrrence of חרשׁ, the verb means to be or remain silent.

There is a third alternative. The LXX of Zephaniah 3:17 reads, "he will renew you," which suggests the confusion of letters *dalet* and *resh* and an underlying Hebrew text with the *piel* of חרש (as in NET and NASB text notes). Renewal certainly fits the context. And what a wonderful thing when our father shouts to the world with joy—about us! Such joy of Yahweh may well give us strength (cf. Neh 8:10).

Brian L. Webster

Made for Praise

ZEPHANIAH 3:20

MT	ESV
בָּעֵת הַהִיא אָבִיא אֶתְכֶם וּבָעֵת קַבְּצִי אֶתְכֶם כִּי־אֶתֵּן אֶתְכֶם לְשֵׁם וְלִתְהִלָּה בְּכֹל עַמֵּי הָאָרֶץ בְּשׁוּבִי אֶת־שְׁבוּתֵיכֶם לְעֵינֵיכֶם אָמַר יְהוָה׃	"At that time I will bring you in, at the time when I gather you together; for I will make you renowned and praised among all the peoples of the earth, when I restore your fortunes before your eyes," says the LORD.

With the shadows of divine judgment looming, Yahweh uses the prophet Zephaniah to muster tireless trust in God's faithfulness to preserve and ultimately satisfy his believing remnant. One of the greatest motivations Zephaniah provides for "seeking" and "waiting for" God (2:3; 3:8) comes in his glorious vision of hope that is held out for all who persevere in faith.

Part of this promise is found in the last verse (3:20), which begins בָּעֵת הַהִיא—specifically, "at that time" of the day of the Lord (3:8) when Yahweh removes the proud and preserves the God-dependent (3:11–13), when the saving king's irreversible victory gives rise to shouts of joy from those rescued (3:14–15), and when Yahweh both delivers and takes delight in his remnant (3:16–19). "At that time" Yahweh will rally his redeemed together for a key reason: כִּי־אֶתֵּן אֶתְכֶם לְשֵׁם וְלִתְהִלָּה בְּכֹל עַמֵּי הָאָרֶץ. The NASB, ESV, and NIV all treat the admiration and acclaim (שֵׁם "name" and תְּהִלָּה "praise") as something the remnant of Judah receives from the onlooking world: "I will give you renown/honor and praise among all the peoples of the earth" (NASB/NIV); "I will make you renowned and praised among all the peoples of the earth" (ESV). Elsewhere, God promises to exalt his own before the world's eyes. Fulfilling their original mission, his people will stand as a kingdom of priests and a holy nation, mediating and displaying God's greatness to the world (Exod 19:5–6; 1 Pet 2:9), and God will give them a new and exalted name (Gen 12:2; Isa 56:5; 62:2; 65:15; 66:22).

However, this text does not simply say that Yahweh will give his redeemed fame and acclaim. Instead, using the לְ preposition, the verse declares that Yahweh will set his people in the center of the world "*for* a name and *for* praise" (לְשֵׁם וְלִתְהִלָּה). Whose name and whose praise is at the fore? The closest parallel texts suggest that *Yahweh's worth and honor* is the ultimate goal of the new creation. It is God's name, God's fame that is to be exalted in the lives of his saints. As asserted by Zephaniah's contemporary Jeremiah, Yahweh originally set his people apart in order "that they might be *for me* [לִי] a people, a name, a praise, and a glory, but they would not listen" (Jer 13:11). Nevertheless, in the new covenant, when sins are forgiven and loyalty is enabled, Yahweh declares that his people "shall be to me [לִי] a name of joy, a praise and a glory before all the nations of the earth" (Jer 33:9). That is, as Ezekiel later testifies, by Yahweh's doing a transforming work within his people by his spirit before the eyes of the nations, he will act "for the sake of my holy name" (Ezek 36:22–23).

The ultimate end of new covenant transformation is worship. All things are from God, through God, and *to God* (Rom 11:36). The new creation, now inaugurated through Christ and his church (2 Cor 5:17; Gal 6:15), is about God. It is about his glory, his Son, his greatness, his exaltation among the peoples of the planet. May your life be marked by the matchless worth of God in Christ, that all "may see your good works and give glory to your Father who is in heaven" (Matt 5:16).

Jason S. DeRouchie

Running to Our Own Houses

MT	NIV
פָּנֹה אֶל־הַרְבֵּה	"You expected much,
וְהִנֵּה לִמְעָט	but see, it turned out to be little.
וַהֲבֵאתֶם הַבַּיִת וְנָפַחְתִּי בוֹ	What you brought home, I blew away.
יַעַן מֶה	Why?"
נְאֻם יְהוָה צְבָאוֹת	declares the LORD Almighty.
יַעַן בֵּיתִי אֲשֶׁר־הוּא חָרֵב	"Because of my house, which remains a ruin,
וְאַתֶּם רָצִים אִישׁ לְבֵיתוֹ׃	while each of you is busy with his own house."

Haggai focuses on the need for the people to rebuild Yahweh's temple since that building project has stalled out. Instead, the people have been focusing on their own houses, leaving the temple (God's house) in ruins. In 1:4 Yahweh, through Haggai, indicts the people who have created rich coverings for their own houses but ignored God's house. Haggai 1:5–6 describes the emptiness of the people's current lives, where they have planted much but found the yield did not match their planting. Haggai 1:9 explains why.

The words "see" (הִנֵּה) and "why?" (מֶה) play an important rhetorical role in this verse. Yahweh is drawing the people's attention to the emptiness of their endeavors by saying, "Pay attention" (הִנֵּה), and then anticipating their question back to him of "why" this is happening to them.

The second half of v. 9 provides a clear answer: the people have neglected God's house and instead cared only for their own. The power of this answer comes in several ways. First, the word "house" (בַּיִת) is used twice but with a different pronominal suffix for each usage, creating the distinction between the treatment of "my house" (בֵּיתִי, i.e., Yahweh's house) compared to each person's own "house" (בֵּיתוֹ). This double use of "house" (בַּיִת) creates a great contrast between the person's choice for their own home rather than God's.

A second means of emphasis is usually missed by English translations because it is a common phrase in Hebrew but is often not fully translatable in English. It is the explicit second personal plural pronoun with *waw*, וְאַתֶּם ("and/but you") in the last line. The Hebrew phrase first emphasizes "you" and then says what "you" do, namely, that "each one runs to his own house." This concept of "running" uses the *qal* participle masculine plural to provide a picture of people running continually toward their homes rather than Yahweh's. One of the functions of a participle is to indicate a continuous action. Haggai is not describing a one-time event; rather, he is explaining that what has kept Yahweh's house in ruins is this continuous action of the people choosing to run to their own homes when they should be running to his home and making it ready.

Verse 10 finishes this answer to the rhetorical question of the people introduced in v. 9. Why has Yahweh blown away what the people brought home? Why do they have so little when they expected to have much? Because their actions of running after their own homes rather than Yahweh's has caused even the heavens and the earth to withhold dew and crops.

We continue in such patterns today, seeking to take care of ourselves and forgetting to tend to God's house. Frequently, we come to realize that the harder we work to "plant" more for our own security, the more it feels like that very security is taken away. We may be tempted to ask "Why?" Haggai 1:9 reminds us that we must seek first God's kingdom, tend first to God's place, and only through this closeness to God do we gain true security.

Beth M. Stovell

Crown Him with How Many Crowns?

ZECHARIAH 6:11–12

MT	NJPS
וְלָקַחְתָּ כֶסֶף־וְזָהָב וְעָשִׂיתָ עֲטָרוֹת וְשַׂמְתָּ בְּרֹאשׁ יְהוֹשֻׁעַ בֶּן־יְהוֹצָדָק הַכֹּהֵן הַגָּדוֹל׃	[11] Take silver and gold and make crowns. Place *one* on the head of High Priest Joshua son of Jehozadak,
וְאָמַרְתָּ אֵלָיו לֵאמֹר כֹּה אָמַר יְהוָה צְבָאוֹת לֵאמֹר הִנֵּה־אִישׁ צֶמַח שְׁמוֹ וּמִתַּחְתָּיו יִצְמָח וּבָנָה אֶת־הֵיכַל יְהוָה׃	[12] and say to him, "Thus said the LORD of Hosts: Behold, a man called the Branch shall branch out from the place where he is, and he shall build the Temple of the LORD."

Zechariah 6:9–15 is an accompanying oracle to the eighth and last vision (6:1–8) of the prophet Zechariah. The symbolic action message depicting the coronation of the high priest Joshua brings to closure the topic of leadership presented in the fourth (ch. 3) and fifth visions (ch. 4). The instructions for the coronation of Joshua are announced in staccato fashion, with the *waw* + suffixing form of the verbs in v. 11 (וְלָקַחְתָּ ... וְעָשִׂיתָ ... וְשַׂמְתָּ), which carry the force of an imperative ("take ... make ... place").

The following messenger formula, "Thus says the LORD of Hosts" (ESV), is better translated, "So said the LORD ..." (NJPS). The *qal* suffixing form of the verb אָמַר indicates past action. The expression suggests the divine assembly or council of gods in ancient Near Eastern thought. The messenger, the Hebrew prophet, stands as an observer in the divine sessions and then only reports what he has heard from God.

The word for crown, עֲטָרָה (v. 11, also in v. 14), is one of three Hebrew words for a crown or tiara (along with נֵזֶר and כֶּתֶר). It describes a crown or a wreath and is not restricted to royalty, since it is worn by persons other than a king (cf. Isa 28:3; Esth 8:15). The plural form of the MT ("crowns") here is difficult, but is the preferred reading (NJPS). The noun probably refers to a double crown or single crown comprised of two circles or bands of metal. Each band represented one of the two offices to which Joshua was appointed (that of king and high priest, contra NJPS). The unifying of the offices of high priest and king in Joshua as the Branch (at least for a time) may anticipate the ultimate joining of those offices in the person of Jesus the Messiah (cf. Heb 7:1, 15). Note the noun "crowns" is omitted (or gapped) but assumed as the direct object in the next clause ("and set [crowns] on the head of Joshua," v. 11b). Neither of the two verses includes direct object markers. This terse style is almost a type of shorthand as the prophet seeks to capture and convey the urgency and significance of the message he has received from Yahweh.

The word צֶמַח ("Branch") is a messianic title (cf. Isa 11:1; Jer 23:5; Zech 3:8). The clause וּמִתַּחְתָּיו יִצְמָח reads literally "from under him he [or one] will sprout up." The compound preposition וּמִתַּחְתָּיו ("from under him") "serves to indicate the future setting of the dynastic hope ... that is to say, ... 'after him,' later on, another Davidide will arise or 'shoot up.'"[1] The high priest Joshua is identified as the Branch, and the one who will rebuild the Second Temple (Zech 6:12–13). Joshua and the Levitical priesthood, at least for a time, will unify the offices of priest and king in postexilic Judah—a remarkable new development in the leadership of Israel—although Zechariah's declaration should not surprise us, since a priest-king ruler after the manner of David and Melchizedek is anticipated in the Psalms (Ps 110:2, 4).

This is a good reminder that God's ways are "unconventional" at times. We need to recognize his divine prerogatives and not let our finely tuned exegetical methods and "canned" theology blind us to the new, to the unexpected, to the marvelous in our triune God's unfolding plan of redemption.

Andrew E. Hill

Notes

1. C. L. Meyers and E. M. Meyers, *Zechariah 1–8* (AB 25B; Garden City, NY: Doubleday, 1987), 355.

Startled by a Visitor

MALACHI 3:1

MT	ESV
הִנְנִי שֹׁלֵחַ מַלְאָכִי וּפִנָּה־דֶרֶךְ לְפָנָי וּפִתְאֹם יָבוֹא אֶל־הֵיכָלוֹ הָאָדוֹן אֲשֶׁר־אַתֶּם מְבַקְשִׁים וּמַלְאַךְ הַבְּרִית אֲשֶׁר־אַתֶּם חֲפֵצִים	"Behold, I send my messenger, and he will prepare the way before me. And the Lord whom you seek will suddenly come to his temple; and the messenger of the covenant in whom you delight, behold, he is coming," says the LORD of hosts.

The unfortunate chapter division beginning Malachi 3 separates God's response to the priests from the description of their corrupt conduct and teaching in ch. 2. According to 2:17, the priests had wearied Yahweh by misrepresenting his character ("Everyone who does evil is good in the sight of the LORD, and he delights in them") and by questioning his ability to exercise justice ("Where is the God of justice?"). Yahweh responds to these delinquent priests in ch. 3.

Several grammatical nuances in Malachi 3:1 suggest that the priests would be surprised, even startled, by Yahweh's response. First, the הִנֵּה at the beginning is likely used to "introduce a new, unsuspected moment" (*HALOT*, 252). Second, the *qal* active participle (שֹׁלֵחַ) suggests "imminent action" (Williams, §214), more literally translated as, "I am *about to send* my messenger," a nuance lacking in the English translations. This nuance conveys the immediacy of Yahweh's response to the priests who have questioned his ability to administer justice—this messenger will prepare the way before the Lord's coming. Third, the next phrase is emphatic and startling—"the Lord ... will suddenly come into his temple." The word "Lord" (אָדוֹן) occurs out of sequence syntactically, at the end of the phrase, in order to emphasize who indeed is coming. In two parallel phrases "the Lord" is equated with "the messenger of the covenant"; they are one and the same person. Each of these terms is modified by an אֲשֶׁר clause: (1) "the Lord *whom* you have been seeking" contains a second person plural personal pronoun (אַתֶּם) and the participle "seeking" (מְבַקְשִׁים), which suggests "continual or repeated action" (Williams, §213); and (2) "the messenger of the covenant *whom* you are desiring" contains a second person plural personal pronoun plus a plural adjective. The attributive adjective in the latter clause assigns the characteristic "desiring" to the pronoun it modifies.

The irony is that even though the priests claim to be "seeking him" and "desiring him," when the coming Lord arrives he will begin a "day of refining" (3:3–4) that they are not anticipating, and it will start with them. These priests had been going through the motions of religious duty, teaching and performing sacrifices, but as 2:8 says, "they have turned aside from the way" and "caused many to stumble." It's a sad day when God's messengers, whose job is to lead people in the ways of God, are hindering that process more than helping it. Reading the list of sins in ch. 2 makes one wonder how they could ever have sunk so low. I believe that the answer is gradually—we who are God's messengers are in greater peril of this problem than anyone, because we can grow accustomed to his Word and in time begin to question it.

I wonder if we need to stop and reflect. As a student, teacher, or pastor, does my instruction match my lifestyle? Does it bring my listeners closer to God rather than away from him? One of these days our ultimate inspector is coming. Will we be caught off guard like these priests?

Paul D. Wegner

Entering the Holy Place

PSALM 1

MT	NIV
אַשְׁרֵי־הָאִישׁ	[1] Blessed is the one
אֲשֶׁר לֹא הָלַךְ בַּעֲצַת רְשָׁעִים	who does not walk in step with the wicked
וּבְדֶרֶךְ חַטָּאִים לֹא עָמָד	or stand in the way that sinners take
וּבְמוֹשַׁב לֵצִים לֹא יָשָׁב:	or sit in the company of mockers,
כִּי אִם בְּתוֹרַת יְהוָה חֶפְצוֹ	[2] but whose delight is in the law of the LORD,
וּבְתוֹרָתוֹ יֶהְגֶּה יוֹמָם וָלָיְלָה:	and who meditates on his law day and night.
וְהָיָה כְּעֵץ שָׁתוּל עַל־פַּלְגֵי מָיִם	[3] That person is like a tree planted by streams of water,
אֲשֶׁר פִּרְיוֹ יִתֵּן בְּעִתּוֹ	which yields its fruit in season
וְעָלֵהוּ לֹא־יִבּוֹל	and whose leaf does not wither—
וְכֹל אֲשֶׁר־יַעֲשֶׂה יַצְלִיחַ:	whatever they do prospers.
לֹא־כֵן הָרְשָׁעִים	[4] Not so the wicked!
כִּי אִם־כַּמֹּץ	They are like chaff
אֲשֶׁר־תִּדְּפֶנּוּ רוּחַ:	that the wind blows away.
עַל־כֵּן לֹא־יָקֻמוּ רְשָׁעִים בַּמִּשְׁפָּט	[5] Therefore the wicked will not stand in the judgment,
וְחַטָּאִים בַּעֲדַת צַדִּיקִים:	nor sinners in the assembly of the righteous.
כִּי־יוֹדֵעַ יְהוָה דֶּרֶךְ צַדִּיקִים	[6] For the LORD watches over the way of the righteous,
וְדֶרֶךְ רְשָׁעִים תֹּאבֵד:	but the way of the wicked leads to destruction.

From at least the time of Jerome (c. AD 347–420), theologians have compared the Psalms to the sanctuary. After all, one went to the sanctuary to come into the presence of God, and the book of Psalms is a collection of prayers and songs spoken in his presence. In fact, this book was the hymnbook of God's people.

If Psalms is like a sanctuary, then, as Jerome and many others have commented, Psalm 1 is the entry into this literary sanctuary. It reflects on the difference between the godly and the ungodly. As we read the psalm as a mirror of our soul (Calvin), we discover whether we are on the road to godliness and righteousness or moving away from God.

The psalm opens with a magnificent example of a three-part parallel line, parallelism being one of the most pervasive conventions of Hebrew poetry. The last two parts (or cola) do not say the same thing, but rather sharpen the thought of the first colon. Moving from walking to standing to sitting, the poet intensifies the potential association between a person and evil. As he moves from "wicked" to "sinners" to "mockers," he uses labels of ever-increasing evil. Of course, the blessed person does not associate with an evil person in any way. The bottom line is that the poet blesses (אַשְׁרֵי is "a petrified plural noun found only in construct phrases")[1] those who do not associate in any serious way with those who are evil.

After such a negative characterization, v. 2, which presents the second parallel line, signals an antithesis with the conjunction כִּי אִם ("but") and positively characterizes the blessed person as one who constantly ("day" and "night" form a merism that means "all the time") studies and reflects on the Torah.

The poet attracts us to wise, righteous, and godly behavior by talking about the consequences, using the metaphor of a tree planted by water. In the same way that a well-watered tree will flourish, so will the godly person.

Verse 4 opens the second stanza with a change of subject

from the blessed righteous person to the wicked person. The shift is abrupt and is signaled by the negative particle לֹא and the adverbial deictic element כֵן ("Not so ..."). The wicked are the opposite of the righteous. If the latter are like a well-watered and productive tree representing life, the wicked are like rootless, dry chaff that represents death. As a result, the wicked will not be counted among the righteous at the time of judgment.

The final stanza is a single verse (v. 6) that summarizes the two preceding stanzas. The form of the parallelism is antithetical, speaking first about the way of the righteous and then the way of the wicked. The *way* (דֶּרֶךְ) is a well-known wisdom motif that stands for one's life. There are only two possible ways: the way of the wise, godly, righteous person that leads to life, and the way of the foolish, wicked, ungodly person that leads to death.

Psalm 1 invites us to introspection, compelling us to ask ourselves which of the two paths are we on. Are we on the way of the righteous or the way of the wicked? Do we avoid associations with wicked people and their behaviors? Do we meditate and study the Scriptures? Psalm 1 urges us to seek God's blessing by following the way of righteousness.

Tremper Longman III

Notes

1. Bruce K. Waltke and Michael P. O'Connor, *An Introduction to Biblical Hebrew Syntax* (Winona Lake, IN: Eisenbrauns, 1990), 681.

Worthy to Be Praised

MT	NIV
רַנְּנוּ צַדִּיקִים בַּיהוָה	[1] Sing joyfully to the Lᴏʀᴅ, you righteous;
לַיְשָׁרִים נָאוָה תְהִלָּה:	it is fitting for the upright to praise him.
הוֹדוּ לַיהוָה בְּכִנּוֹר	[2] Praise the Lᴏʀᴅ with the harp;
בְּנֵבֶל עָשׂוֹר זַמְּרוּ־לוֹ:	make music to him on the ten-stringed lyre.
שִׁירוּ־לוֹ שִׁיר חָדָשׁ	[3] Sing to him a new song;
הֵיטִיבוּ נַגֵּן בִּתְרוּעָה:	play skillfully, and shout for joy.
כִּי־יָשָׁר דְּבַר־יְהוָה	[4] For the word of the Lᴏʀᴅ is right and true;
וְכָל־מַעֲשֵׂהוּ בֶּאֱמוּנָה:	he is faithful in all he does.
אֹהֵב צְדָקָה וּמִשְׁפָּט	[5] The Lᴏʀᴅ loves righteousness and justice;
חֶסֶד יְהוָה מָלְאָה הָאָרֶץ:	the earth is full of his unfailing love.

Psalm 33 is a beautiful psalm of praise. The psalmist opens with an invocation to sing praise to Yahweh (vv. 1–3). The reasons why God should be praised quickly follow in vv. 4–5: "For [כִּי] the word of the LORD is right and true; he is faithful in all he does. The LORD loves righteousness and justice; the earth is full of his unfailing love."

These two verses contain a number of theologically rich words, including יָשָׁר ,אֱמוּנָה ,צְדָקָה ,מִשְׁפָּט, and חֶסֶד. All are common in the psalms and are used frequently in conjunction with one another. Their usage in Psalm 33, moreover, provides an excellent opportunity for word study. Through synchronic analysis of these key Hebrew terms,[1] we can better understand the meaning of Psalm 33:1–5.

According to v. 4, "the word of the LORD is right and true; he is faithful in all he does." God often accomplishes his purposes simply by speaking, and his speech is entirely יָשָׁר, or upright and without blame. Everything God does, moreover, is done in אֱמוּנָה; he always acts in a faithful and truthful manner and is, therefore, reliable. Together, יָשָׁר and אֱמוּנָה represent God's character, evident through his speech and actions. God never lies or acts wrongly (cf. Deut 32:4).

The phrase צְדָקָה וּמִשְׁפָּט in v. 5 (NIV "righteousness and justice") is a hendiadys, or a single idea expressed through two words. Righteousness and justice are often thought of as spiritual terms, and rightfully so, but together they can have the connotation of "social justice" (e.g., 2 Sam 8:15; 1 Kgs 10:9; Ps 99:4; Jer 22:3, 15). Here, Yahweh is concerned with ensuring that the wrongs of this world are made right and that social justice is achieved.[2]

Lastly, חֶסֶד (NIV "unfailing love") most frequently occurs with reference to God, describing the effects of divine חֶסֶד toward humanity: God rescues people from disaster, sustains life, forgives sin, and shows mercy. According to the psalmist here, Yahweh's חֶסֶד is abundant and fills the earth (v. 5)! The totality expressed here parallels the totality of Yahweh's faithfulness mentioned in v. 4.

It can be difficult to capture the essence of all the above-discussed "big" words in Psalm 33:4–5. Nevertheless, synchronic analysis of their usage in the Hebrew Bible can give us a clearer picture of what these two verses mean. Yahweh always speaks and acts uprightly, he desires for righteousness and justice to be attained at the spiritual as well as the societal level, and our very existence owes itself to his unfailing love.

Our God is certainly a God worthy to be worshiped! Let us join the psalmist, therefore, in praising Yahweh.

Benjamin J. Noonan

Notes

1. See John H. Walton, "Principles for Productive Word Study," *NIDOTTE*, 1:161–71.

2. Cf. Christopher J. H. Wright, *Old Testament Ethics for the People of God* (Downers Grove, IL: InterVarsity, 2004), 255–57.

A Penitential Devotional

PSALM 51:3–4 [ENGLISH 51:1–2]

MT	KJV
חָנֵּנִי אֱלֹהִים	[1] Have mercy upon me, O God,
כְּחַסְדֶּךָ	according to thy lovingkindness:
כְּרֹב רַחֲמֶיךָ	according unto the multitude of thy tender mercies
מְחֵה פְשָׁעָי:	blot out my transgressions.
הֶרֶב כַּבְּסֵנִי מֵעֲוֹנִי	[2] Wash me thoroughly from mine iniquity,
וּמֵחַטָּאתִי טַהֲרֵנִי:	and cleanse me from my sin.

Psalm 51, called "the Psalm of all Psalms," teaches us how we can restore our relationship with God when we defraud, lie, cheat, gossip, and do other sins that people do.

When David composed this exemplary penitential psalm, he had committed adultery with Bathsheba and murdered her husband, Uriah. The law mandated David's death for both (Num 35:29–20; Deut 22:23–24). Nevertheless, through this psalm he found forgiveness and cleansing and instructs all of us how to be restored in our relationship with God (see v. 15 [v. 13]):

His prefatory petition in vv. 3–4 [1–2] tells us how in a nutshell. First, he confesses his sins: "*my* transgressions." His three words for sin almost exhaust the Hebrew vocabulary: "sin" (חַטָּאת), "iniquity" (עָוֹן), and "transgression" (פֶּשַׁע). "Sin" is the most basic word; it means a disqualifying offense against someone with whom you have a relationship. "Iniquity" is the most holistic term, encompassing both the crime and its guilt. "Transgression" is the strongest term, "a willful, knowledgeable violation of the norm/standard." Every word assumes God's law has been violated. So David says in v. 6 [4]: "Against thee, thee only, have I sinned." Therefore, if God says we are forgiven, we are forgiven, even if others do not. "Whoever conceals their sins does not prosper, but the one who confesses and renounces them finds mercy" (Prov 28:13 NIV).

Second, standing in the dark, deep hole of sin, the inspired psalmist looks up and sees three stars of God's grace that those who stand in the noonday sunlight of their own righteousness never see: "mercy," "lovingkindness," and "tender mercies." The Hebrew word for "have mercy" (חנן) — better, "be gracious" — means "bestow a favor that cannot be claimed." The word for "lovingkindness" (חֶסֶד) means "help for the helpless." Joseph could not bury himself in the Promised Land, and so he depended on the "lovingkindness" of his brothers to bury his bones there. "Tender mercy" (רַחֲמִים) denotes the tender affections of a superior for a helpless inferior, as a mother for her child.

Finally, notice his bold, double petition: "blot out" and "wash me." "Blot out" (מחה) means "to wipe clean" (a dish, mouth, or tears); "to obliterate" (a writing or remembrance of some sort). This imagery draws on the way kings kept record of the events in their realm. So, God has entirely erased the penitent believer's crime from his ledger.

But David wants more than a legal forgiveness; he also wants to have his conscience cleansed. He feels like dirty underwear and stinks up the place wherever he goes. So he asks, "wash me" (כבס). The Hebrew means "to launder"; it refers to treading, kneading, or beating to make the garment clean with lye and soap.

But how can God erase the crime and launder our consciences and at the same time be just? Either the sinner must die or justice must die. David resolves the tension in v. 9 [7]: "Purge [חטא *piel*, lit., "De-sin"] me with hyssop, and I shall be clean." He is alluding to two liturgical rituals that cleanse by filling the hairy plant with blood and water and by sprinkling: the leper's house (Lev 14:49, 52) and that of a person defiled by a corpse. The Targum, an ancient Aramaic interpretive translation of the Hebrew text, paraphrases: "Sprinkle on me as the priest who sprinkles with hyssop the blood of the sacrifice of the leper or the water of the ashes of the red heifer on the person defiled." These atoning sacrifices foreshadow the sacrifice of Christ for us (Heb 9:11 – 14); he died in our place.

Come boldly, penitent sinner, to God's throne of grace, confess your sin and trust the blood of Jesus Christ to cleanse you of your sin.

Bruce Waltke

Speak Truth
JOB 42:7b

MT	NIV
כִּי לֹא דִבַּרְתֶּם אֵלַי נְכוֹנָה כְּעַבְדִּי אִיּוֹב:	Because you have not spoken the truth about me, as my servant Job has.

The Hebrew in Job is among the most challenging in the canon to render into English; an array of varying translations of the book confirms its difficulty. Of the many textual nuances throughout the book, careful rendering of a single, ubiquitous preposition in ch. 42 provides the reader with a clearer understanding of the magnificent closure to the book.

In 42:7b, repeated in v. 8b, Yahweh addresses Job's friends, who throughout the book offer consolation and advice to their desperate comrade. You may recall that while the friends fault Job for his misfortunes, they laud Yahweh as just and mighty. Eliphaz proclaims, "He saves the needy from the sword in their mouth; he saves them from the clutches of the powerful. So the poor have hope, and injustice shuts its mouth" (5:15–16). Bildad states, "Surely God does not reject one who is blameless or strengthen the hands of evildoers" (8:20). And Zophar questions Job, "Can you fathom the mysteries of God? Can you probe the limits of the Almighty?" (11:7).

In 42:7, Yahweh addresses Eliphaz and his two friends in anger since apparently they did *not* speak the truth "about" him. There seems to be a contradiction here. Why did God deem such claims as "dominion and awe belong to God; he establishes order in the heights of heaven" (25:2) untruthful? If anything, Job appears to be the one advocating questionable truth "about" God, stating, "God's terrors are marshaled against me" (6:4b). There is another explanation here that makes more sense, one that relies on a different rendering of the Hebrew preposition אֶל.

English translations have rendered the preposition אֶל in 42:7b as "about" (NIV, CEB) and "of" (NAS, NRSV), interpreting the particle to provide specification to something otherwise ambiguously stated. This is one of the many uses of אֶל throughout the Hebrew Bible. Yet contextually this is not the best interpretation. This preposition is also frequently used declaratively, to mark the recipient of a verb of speech. This, I propose, provides the best translation of the particle in the context of 42:7b. My translation, then, varies just slightly, "Because you have not spoken the truth *to* me, as my servant Job has," but its meaning is pivotal. The fault in Job's friends is not that they have not spoken words of truth "about" God; rather, they did not speak truthfully "to" him, at least not as Job did. The distinction provides sweet clarity for the reader of this heavy narrative. Yahweh's anger against the friends deals more specifically with the heart. Job spoke to Yahweh truthfully, from a broken heart, an angered heart, one of desperation, one of gloom, one that wished to give up. Consider Job's words:

> "Why have you made me your target? Have I become a burden to you?" (7:20b)
> "I loathe my very life; therefore I will give free rein to my complaint and speak out in the bitterness of my soul." (10:1)
> "My face is red with weeping, dark shadows ring my eyes." (16:16a)

The biblical corpus supports this honest, truthful bringing to Yahweh. Jeremiah, too, questions God, "Why is my pain unending and my wound grievous and incurable? You are to me like a deceptive brook, like a spring that fails" (Jer 15:18). Yet Yahweh's response brings the prophet gentle comfort, "For I am with you to rescue and save you" (15:20b). In a culture where we have difficulty being real even with ourselves, and perhaps even more so with those around us, might we not take great encouragement from our heroes of faith who, like Job, spoke honestly and truthfully *to* our deity? Oh, that we too might ever be real to him!

Nancy L. Erickson

For Gaining Wisdom

PROVERBS 1:1–7

MT	NIV
מִשְׁלֵי שְׁלֹמֹה בֶן־דָּוִד מֶלֶךְ יִשְׂרָאֵל:	[1] The proverbs of Solomon son of David, king of Israel:
לָדַעַת חָכְמָה וּמוּסָר	[2] for gaining wisdom and instruction;
לְהָבִין אִמְרֵי בִינָה:	for understanding words of insight;
לָקַחַת מוּסַר הַשְׂכֵּל	[3] for receiving instruction in prudent behavior,
צֶדֶק וּמִשְׁפָּט וּמֵישָׁרִים:	doing what is right and just and fair;
לָתֵת לִפְתָאיִם עָרְמָה	[4] for giving prudence to those who are simple,
לְנַעַר דַּעַת וּמְזִמָּה:	knowledge and discretion to the young—
יִשְׁמַע חָכָם וְיוֹסֶף לֶקַח	[5] let the wise listen and add to their learning,
וְנָבוֹן תַּחְבֻּלוֹת יִקְנֶה:	and let the discerning get guidance—
לְהָבִין מָשָׁל וּמְלִיצָה	[6] for understanding proverbs and parables,
דִּבְרֵי חֲכָמִים וְחִידֹתָם:	the sayings and riddles of the wise.
יִרְאַת יְהוָה רֵאשִׁית דָּעַת	[7] The fear of the LORD is the beginning of knowledge,
חָכְמָה וּמוּסָר אֱוִילִים בָּזוּ:	but fools despise wisdom and instruction.

The book of Proverbs contains a collection of discourses (1:8–9:18) as well as proverbs (chs. 10–31) that come preeminently from Solomon (see 1:1, though see also 22:27; 24:23; 25:1; 30:1). The first seven verses form the preface, which orients us to reading the book in a way that maximizes the benefits we can gain from the collected wisdom of the sages.

The most striking syntactical feature of these verses is the extensive use of the infinitive construct with a prefixed *lamed* (לְ) at the beginning of most of the five two-part parallel lines or bi-cola (vv. 2a, 2b, 3a, 4a, and 6a). This form indicates purpose, so if we want to discover what Proverbs is about, we must pay attention to these phrases.

The first of the five purpose phrases is the most general. The proverbs are for "gaining wisdom and instruction" (v. 2a). What is wisdom and instruction? First, it is a practical skill of living, as becomes clear in other contexts where this word (חָכְמָה) is used (Exod 28:3; 31:6; Prov 24:3). Do you want success at work and a vibrant life with a happy family and good friends? Proverbs will point the way. Do you want to stay away from the behaviors and attitudes that lead to failure? Proverbs will warn you what to avoid. Indeed, the second purpose phrase ("for understanding words of insight," v. 2b) tells us that not only does Proverbs impart wisdom, but it helps us to gain the ability to understand and apply these sayings (see also v. 6).

At first, the third purpose phrase (v. 3a) appears simply to repeat the thought of the first two and the fifth, though perhaps with more emphasis on the perspective of the reader or student. However, closer examination shows that the second colon ("doing what is right and just and fair") takes wisdom to the next level. The wisdom of Proverbs is not only practical; it's ethical. The wise are not only skillful; they are righteous.

While the first three purpose phrases speak from the perspective of the student, the fourth (v. 4a) comes from that of the teacher, the one who imparts wisdom to others. The wisdom of the book is for the "simple," who are also characterized as "young." Those familiar with the book of Proverbs will not be surprised here, since the discourses in chs. 1–9 are often addressed by a father to his son. The term "simple" here is best understood as immature, though the term may imply a bent toward foolishness, since "folly is bound up in the heart of a child" (22:15). What is surprising is that the audience is larger than just immature young men. The parenthetical statement in v. 5 uses jussives to point out that, though the book may directly address the immature young, it is even for the wise. Proverbs is important for everyone to read!

This preface prepares us for this book by telling us that its purpose is for us to gain wisdom and the ability to understand wise sayings and to apply them to our lives. Wisdom is not only practical; it is also ethical. According to the final verse of the preface, the foundation of wisdom is theological. One cannot even start being wise unless one has the proper relationship with God, a relationship characterized by "fear."

Why fear? The Hebrew word (from the root ירא) does not denote the type of fear that makes one run away. It is the kind of fear that recognizes that it is God, not we, who is the center of the universe. This fear breeds humility and an openness to listen to God's advice about how we should live life as delivered through the book of Proverbs.

Tremper Longman III

Warning: Seduction at Work!

PROVERBS 25:15

MT	NJPS
בְּאֹרֶךְ אַפַּיִם יְפֻתֶּה קָצִין	Through forbearance a ruler may be won over;
וְלָשׁוֹן רַכָּה תִּשְׁבָּר־גָּרֶם׃	A gentle tongue can break bones.

Proverbs 25:15 is usually explained as counseling patience: "To the other virtues the pedagogic proverb adds gentleness."[1] In support of this reading, the root פתה is explained as "*presumably* having a *positive* sense [in Prov. 25:15] to persuade someone through speech to do the wise, not the foolish, thing."[2]

When lexical explanations use words like "rare" "or "presumably," we ought to read with caution, especially when an allegedly "rare" function is invoked to support or "prove" a rendering. Even when there is a consistent tradition of interpretation and translation, we need to test whether a "unique" or "presumed" function is in fact taking place.

Every other occurrence of the verb פתה in the Hebrew Bible (apart from this verse) describes seducing or tricking someone to act to his or her disadvantage (e.g., 2 Sam 3:25; 1 Kgs 22:20–22 [par. 2 Chr 18:19–21]; Ps 78:36; Prov 1:10; 16:29).[3] It describes, for example, sexual seduction (Exod 22:16 [Eng. 15]; Deut 11:16; Judg 14:15; 16:5; Job 31:9), YHWH's sending a spirit to "seduce" Ahab to fight and be killed (1 Kgs 22:20–22; par. 2 Chr 18:19–21), and Jeremiah's complaint that YHWH had "seduced" him into becoming a prophet (Jer 20:7, 10).

This also explains the meaning of the "simple" in Proverbs (where the root פתה is most frequent): the naïve (פֶּתִי) can be seduced because they lack the knowledge and understanding that experience brings (e.g., Prov 1:22, 32; 7:7; 8:5; 9:4, 16).

Most of the verses in Proverbs 25 are "emblematic" proverbs—one line draws a "picture" and the other provides its explanatory "caption," usually in that order (e.g., 25:3, 4–5, 6–7, 11–12). In v. 15, however, the pattern is reversed: the emblem—"a soft tongue breaks a bone"—is the second line (the Hebrew does not say or imply "can" or "may").

Proverbs 25:15b is often criticized because tongues do not lick their way through bones. We can, however, read this in at least two other ways: as either hyperbole or metonymy, both of which fit the poetic nature of gnomic literature. Hyperbole (deliberate exaggeration for effect) would imply that we've never seen this happen, but that's how it works: as slowly and patiently as a dog licking a bone. Metonymy (when a part refers to the whole) suggests that rulers can be seduced into deadly decisions. Then indeed—and quite literally—patient words (the "soft tongue") would break their victim's bone(s).

This interpretation also aligns this saying with the function of the book of Proverbs as a "training manual" for future Israelite leaders—those in positions of authority and therefore people whom others would like to manipulate—just as today it cautions anyone in authority (parents, teachers, politicians, and civic authorities).

Proverbs 25:15 does not commend morally neutral patience; rather, it encourages leaders to consider both the character and motives of their advisors (e.g., to ask why they support certain options). And it reminds them to guard against following the quiet, "sensible" advice that—in the long run—shatters even bone.

Frederic Clarke Putnam

Notes

1. Bruce K. Waltke, *The Book of Proverbs: Chapters 15–31*, NICOT (Grand Rapids: Eerdmans, 2005), 324.

2. Ibid., italics added.

3. "In piel and pual … it means to manipulate a person into a position in which the person is no longer capable of holding his or her ground and as a result comes to harm" (R. Mosis, פתה, *TDOT* 12:170).

Agur's Hebrew Words for "Words"

PROVERBS 30:1

MT	KJV
דִּבְרֵי אָגוּר בִּן־יָקֶה	The words of Agur the son of Jakeh,
הַמַּשָּׂא	even the prophecy:
נְאֻם הַגֶּבֶר לְאִיתִיאֵל	the man spake unto Ithiel,
לְאִיתִיאֵל וְאֻכָל:	even unto Ithiel and Ucal,

Proverbs 30:1 introduces us to a favorite author of mine. We can learn much about Agur just by reflecting on his Hebrew "words" used in the title of his work. I am using the English translation of that title in the KJV. I hope that after reading his autobiography in the three words ("words," "prophecy," and "spake"), you will better understand him.

In English, "word" commonly means the smallest element in a language that may be uttered or written in isolation and carry a meaning; rarely does one word, such as "yes" or "no," express a complete thought. But the Hebrew דָּבָר means a complete thought—what in English would be called "a sentence." In the Hebrew Bible, the Ten Commandments are called "the ten words" (Deut 4:13). That is why the NIV renders the Hebrew here as "The *sayings* of Agur." The sayings are essentially the following verses, which Agur collected in a meaningful word.

When we sit at the feet of Agur, we are listening to the sayings of a wise man.

Agur tells us that his sayings are "a prophecy" (מַשָּׂא). More precisely this term designates a "judgment prophecy." A judgment prophecy normally consists of an accusation for wrong behavior and a just punishment. When you understand that Agur's sayings belong to this literary genre, you read them in a brighter light. The essential thrust of his collected sayings censure greed and hubris, teaching subordination to authority: to God's message (30:1b – 9) in the state and in the home (30:10 – 16), and so to live within boundaries (30:17 – 31). Two of his sayings explicitly threaten judgment for violating his teaching: "Do not slander a servant to their master, or they will curse you, and you will pay for it" (v. 10, NIV), and "the eye that mocks a father, that scorns an aged mother, will be pecked out by the ravens of the valley, will be eaten by the vultures" (v. 17). He concludes his sayings to his son Ithiel with this warning: "If you play the fool and exalt yourself, or if you plan evil, clap your hand over your mouth! For as churning cream produces butter, and as twisting the nose produces blood, so stirring up anger produces strife" (vv. 32 – 33). When we sit at the feet of Agur, we are listening to a prophet with a sober warning of judgment for not living either under God's authority or within his established boundaries.

"Spake" obscures the thought of the Hebrew word נְאֻם. This Hebrew word occurs 365 of 376 times in the expression נְאֻם יְהוָה ("the LORD says"). That phrase signifies that the words that follow originated with Yahweh and carry his authority. Once (Jer 23:31) נְאֻם occurs without a connection to an author and has the same sense. David used this expression in Psalm 110:1: נְאֻם יְהוָה לַאדֹנִי, usually translated "The LORD said to my Lord." But Jesus interpreted the meaning of the Hebrew word when he introduced his citation of this verse: "He said to them [the Pharisees], 'How is it then that David, *speaking by the Spirit*, calls him "Lord"? For he says, "The Lord said to my Lord"'"

(Matt 22:43–44, emphasis mine). The other ten occurrences are connected with a human author to denote the heavenly origin of his utterance and its divine authority: six times of Balaam's oracles (Num 24:3[2x], 4, 15[2x], 16), three times of David's inspired hymns (2 Sam 23:1[2x]; Ps 36:1[2]), and once of Agur's sayings. Remarkably, both Balaam and David use exactly the same expression as Agur: נְאֻם הַגֶּבֶר ("the inspired utterance of the man"). The word translated "man" (גֶּבֶר) means "a strong man, as distinct from woman and children, whom he must defend." When we sit at the feet of Agur, we are listening to the sayings of the Holy Spirit through a strong man.

Space does not permit me to clarify "even unto Ithiel and Ucal." But I hope now that you have met this wise, sobering, and inspiring prophet, you will run, not walk, to hear him.

Bruce Waltke

A Lesson and Exercise in Wisdom through the Animal World

PROVERBS 30:24–28

MT	ESV
אַרְבָּעָה הֵם קְטַנֵּי־אָרֶץ	24 Four things on earth are small
וְהֵמָּה חֲכָמִים מְחֻכָּמִים:	but they are exceedingly wise:
הַנְּמָלִים עַם לֹא־עָז	25 the ants are a people not strong,
וַיָּכִינוּ בַקַּיִץ לַחְמָם:	yet they provide their food in the summer;
שְׁפַנִּים עַם לֹא־עָצוּם	26 the rock badgers are a people not mighty,
וַיָּשִׂימוּ בַסֶּלַע בֵּיתָם:	yet they make their homes in the cliffs;
מֶלֶךְ אֵין לָאַרְבֶּה	27 the locusts have no king,
וַיֵּצֵא חֹצֵץ כֻּלּוֹ:	yet all of them march in rank;
שְׂמָמִית בְּיָדַיִם תְּתַפֵּשׂ	28 the lizard you can take in your hands,
וְהִיא בְּהֵיכְלֵי מֶלֶךְ:	yet it is in kings' palaces.

Proverbs 30:24–28 presents a series of metaphors for depicting how the physically insignificant can be formidable through their wisdom. By metaphorically equating specific, small animals with wise people, this passage reminds us of the importance of wisdom. As believers, we must have both faith and wisdom. The book of Proverbs teaches that wisdom is not only intellect and knowledge but also the power and discipline to apply such intellect and knowledge for success in faithful and righteous living.[1]

Verse 24 employs two nominal clauses, conjoined with a disjunctive *waw*, to introduce the seemingly contradictory observation of how animals (and thus people) can be small yet potent through their wisdom. The succeeding verses present each animal in a riddle-like structure, which is the exegetical focus. With the first three animals, the A line employs a nominal or existential clause to present each animal metaphorically as a physically limited person, and the corresponding B line opens with an epexegetical, gnomic *wayyiqtol* to explain how each animal overcomes its limited strength through wisdom.[2] However, because the B lines provide veiled explanations, the readers are invited to build their wisdom by investigating exactly how each animal uses wisdom, which also provides a deeper understanding of wisdom itself. Ultimately, this passage gives a valuable lesson by reminding us that wisdom must be continually sought, especially through the exercise of our minds.

In v. 25b, the phrase "in the summer" (בַּקַּיִץ) highlights how the ants' inner strength is wisdom expressed through their diligence in the summer, in which they have the good sense to realize that the summer's harvest must provide for the rest of the year. As a result, the ants portray how diligence coupled with good sense yields strength of a different sort.

In v. 26b, the phrase "in the crags" (בַּסֶּלַע, "in the cliffs," ESV) emphasizes how special skills are necessary for building houses in high rocky areas, which are commonly understood as fortresses (note סֶלַע in Ps 71:3; Jer 49:16). Moreover, the usage of the metonymy—physical house (בֵּיתָם, "homes" ESV) for the inhabitants of the house—portrays how the badgers' special skill in rockwork provides a mighty fortress that establishes a mighty house (family). Whereas great dynastic families are usually a product of military strength, this proverb shows how technical skill from wisdom can achieve the same end.

In v. 27b, "in rank" (חֹצֵץ), an adverbial accusative of manner, focuses on how wisdom can provide instruction and order. Although locusts congregate in vast numbers, they can only be an overpowering force because they intuitively know how to function as a totality; that is, the locusts need no king (i.e., military commander) since they have wisdom functioning as their king.

In v. 28 the author signals the end of the passage by inverting the expected structure of nominal/existential clause + finite verbal clause. The contrast between the lizard's vulnerability to capture and its ability to infiltrate palaces portrays how the wise possess cunning that allows them to penetrate strongholds without recourse to physical power.

Kevin Chau

Notes

1. Michael V. Fox, *Proverbs 1–9: A New Translation with Introduction and Commentary*, AB 18A (New York: Doubleday, 2000), 33.

2. The more common usage of the *wayyiqtol* is for temporal and logical consecution, but the epexegetical usage (explication) often follows nominal constructions. See Bruce K. Waltke and Michael P. O'Connor, *An Introduction to Biblical Hebrew Syntax* (Winona Lake, IN: Eisenbrauns, 1990), sec. 32.2.2, 33.3.4.

The Faith Commitment of a Moabite

MT	NET
וַתֹּאמֶר רוּת אַל־תִּפְגְּעִי־בִי לְעָזְבֵךְ לָשׁוּב מֵאַחֲרָיִךְ כִּי אֶל־אֲשֶׁר תֵּלְכִי אֵלֵךְ וּבַאֲשֶׁר תָּלִינִי אָלִין עַמֵּךְ עַמִּי וֵאלֹהַיִךְ אֱלֹהָי׃	But Ruth replied, "Stop urging me to abandon you! For wherever you go, I will go. Wherever you live, I will live. Your people will become my people, and your God will become my God."

This passage in the book of Ruth is familiar to most readers of the Old Testament. It is recognized as a statement of loyalty to Naomi by Ruth, and it serves as an example of human faithfulness to us today.

But something more profound is going on here than some English translations reveal. In the NET translation above, the idea expressed is that Naomi's people will *become* Ruth's people, and that Naomi's God, Yahweh, will *become* Ruth's God. That is, these are things that are yet to happen from Ruth's perspective.

The Hebrew will support other interpretations. There is a shift from the imperfect ("where you go, *I will* go and where you lodge, *I will* lodge," אֶל־אֲשֶׁר תֵּלְכִי אֵלֵךְ וּבַאֲשֶׁר תָּלִינִי אָלִין) to verbless sentences in which the verb "to be" must be supplied (lit., "your people my people, your God my God," עַמֵּךְ עַמִּי וֵאלֹהַיִךְ אֱלֹהָי). It is possible that the future sense of the imperfects is intended to be carried over to the verbless sentences (as in the NET translation above). But it is also possible that the author of Ruth is deliberately shifting to verbless sentences to describe something that is a present reality, not something yet to come. In that case, we would translate the verbless sentences as "your people *are* my people and your God *is* my God."

The previous verse gives a clue as to how the author may have intended Ruth's declaration to be understood. Verse 15 says, " 'Look,' said Naomi, 'your sister-in-law is going back to her people *and her gods*. Go back with her.' " Ruth's choice to stay with Naomi is a surprising one from an ancient Near Eastern perspective. Her future would have been far more secure had she returned to her father's house and sought a second husband from among her people, the Moabites. But returning to her father's house would also have meant worshiping her father's gods, such as Chemosh, the god of the Moabites. That is something Ruth simply could not do if she had committed herself to following Yahweh and had accepted that he is the one true God. Unlike her sister-in-law, Ruth takes a radically countercultural step because her faith in Yahweh will not allow her to do otherwise. Her declaration is not that she *intends* to commit herself to Yahweh, but that she already *has*.

We should also consider how Ruth came to understand who Yahweh is such that she could make this countercultural move. It had to be from Naomi and her family. Thus, in the midst of the dark days of the judges (Ruth is set in "the days when the judges judged," Ruth 1:1), one family among God's people, at least, was living in such a way as to reveal who God is and to invite others into relationship with him on the basis of their witness. This is just as the people of God—in Ruth's day as well as our own—are called to do!

Peter Vogt

The Plural of Love

SONG OF SONGS 1:2; 5:1b

MT	NIV
יִשָּׁקֵנִי מִנְּשִׁיקוֹת פִּיהוּ	1:2 Let him kiss me with the kisses of his mouth—
כִּי־טוֹבִים דֹּדֶיךָ מִיָּיִן׃	for your love is more delightful than wine.
אִכְלוּ רֵעִים שְׁתוּ וְשִׁכְרוּ דּוֹדִים׃	5:1b Eat, friends, and drink; drink your fill of love.

The Song of Songs, meaning "the best song," is one of the most difficult books in the Bible to interpret. When was it written? Who wrote it? To whom was it written? What is it about? Why is it in our Bible? Questions like these are fundamental to interpretation, but few agree on the answers. Anyone who has worked with the Hebrew text of this song will be familiar with an additional set of difficulties. For example, there are fifty-seven different words in this book that appear nowhere else in the Hebrew Bible. Forty-five of these words occur only once (*hapax legomenon*), and this can make identification of meaning difficult to achieve. Or, compare a variety of English translations for Song of Songs 6:12. There are moments, however, when through careful study we can take a small step forward in understanding this sensational song. The use of the noun דּוֹד ("beloved, lover, uncle") provides a good example.

The Hebrew noun דּוֹד occurs sixty-one times in the Hebrew

Bible (fifty-one times in the singular, ten times in the plural). The fact that it appears thirty-nine times in the Song of Songs is significant in terms of distribution — well over sixty percent of the total occurrences. In terms of meaning, this noun can indicate the family relationship of "uncle" (e.g., Lev 10:4; Num 36:11; 1 Sam 10:14 – 16; 2 Kgs 24:17; Esth 2:7, 15), or, more generically, "love" or someone's "lover" or "beloved" (e.g., Prov 7:18; Isa 5:1; Ezek 16:8; 23:17). The context of the Song of Songs suggests that "uncle" is not the author's intention, but rather the more generic designation of "love," "lover," or "beloved."

It is also important to observe how the author of this song uses the singular and the plural forms of this noun (the plural only in 1:2, 4; 4:10; 5:1; 7:13). The singular form is used most often by the young woman when referring to the one she loves, "My *beloved* belongs to me, and I belong to him" (2:16). The plural form, however, is often translated as the more abstract concept of love, "Let him kiss me with the kisses of his mouth, for your *love* is better than wine" (1:2). But recent advances in our understanding of other Semitic languages related to Hebrew suggest that the plural form of דוד is best translated not as the abstract idea "love," but rather as the act of "lovemaking."[1]

This more precise translation makes perfect sense within the context of the Song of Songs. Consider our two passages. Song of Songs 1:2 might be better translated, "for making love to you is better [i.e., more intoxicating] than wine." Song of Songs 5:1b would read, "Eat, friends, drink and be drunk with lovemaking!"

These revised translations help us to better understand the intent of the author and to clarify the more general subject matter of the book. It is good for us to be reminded that the Bible does not shy away from the joy and pleasure of this one-flesh relationship established by God in creation. In fact, according to Song of Songs, the covenant of marriage should be both rock solid in terms of commitment and white hot in terms of sexual enjoyment (Song 8:6–7). The world has pursued white-hot sexual pleasure without rock-solid commitment. But the church has emphasized rock-solid commitment to the neglect of white-hot sexual pleasure. The Bible, however, holds these two realities together, and so will those of us who want strong marriages that bear the fruit of Edenic pleasure and commitment.

Miles V. Van Pelt

Notes

1. Compare the Akkadian cognate *dādu*, the Ugaritic cognate *dd*, and the Egyptian *dd* with the phallus determinative, each of which is employed to denote activities associated with lovemaking. A similar distinction exists in the singular and plural forms of the Hebrew noun דָּם. In the singular this noun means "blood," but in the plural it can mean "bloodshed" or "bloodguilt."

Breathe In. Breathe Out. Repeat as Needed.

ECCLESIASTES 1:2

MT	NJPS
הֲבֵל הֲבָלִים אָמַר קֹהֶלֶת	Utter futility!—said Koheleth—
הֲבֵל הֲבָלִים הַכֹּל הָבֶל:	Utter futility! All is futile!

Even those with little biblical knowledge know "Vanity of vanities, all is vanity" (Eccl 1:2; 12:8, KJV). Does Qohelet (or Koheleth, as the author calls himself) really mean that everything is pointless? Three aspects of v. 1 deserve a closer look: the phrase *hăbēl hăbālîm* (הֲבֵל הֲבָלִים), the word *hebel* (הֶבֶל) itself, and the one-word phrase *hakkōl* (הַכֹּל) .

First, phrases of the type "X of X's" express the superlative: "the lowest slave" (Gen 9:25), "the holiest [place]" (Exod 26:33), "the highest king" (Ezek 26:7; Dan 2:37), or "the best song" (Song 1:1). The phrase *hăbēl hăbālîm* thus means "the most *hebel*-like of all *hebels*"; something has led Qohelet to conclude that everything is "utmost" or "pure" *hebel*, which leads to the second question: the meaning of *hebel*.

Ecclesiastes is the only biblical book whose interpretation is controlled by the meaning of one word. It is generally read as asserting that nothing is really worthwhile, that everything we do is "meaningless" (NIV). Jerome rendered the Hebrew word *hebel* by the Latin *vanitas* (Vulgate), which became "vanyte" (Wycliffe); this reading has determined the basic approach to the book ever since. But what does the Hebrew word *hebel* really mean?

Lexica and most commentators agree that *hebel* refers to "breath" or "vapor" (cf. Ps 62:9 [English 10]; Prov 21:6; Isa 57:13), but then immediately assert that in Ecclesiastes "breath" is a metaphor for "vanity" or "futility," and so the book implies that "All is absurd."[1] This leap, however, seems neither necessary nor warranted: breath is crucial, not futile. (Try not breathing.) It is, however, ephemeral — here now and gone when we exhale.

Rendering *hebel* as "breath" suggests that Qohelet is not saying that everything is meaningless, but rather that everything — which is important "in its time" (3:1a) — will vanish from "under the sun." (Rendering *hebel* as "vapor" lacks the sense of "crucial to life," but keeps that of ephemerality.)

This understanding of *hebel* makes sense of, for example, "Enjoy happiness with a woman you love all the fleeting days of life [*kol yĕmê ḥayyê heblekā*]" (Eccl 9:9) — love is not "vain" or "meaningless," but it will pass when we die, so enjoy it while God grants it.

Third, outside Ecclesiastes, the phrase *hakkōl* ("everything") usually refers to a contextual list of items, either explicit (e.g., Exod 29:24; Lev 1:9, 13; 1 Kgs 7:33) or implicit (e.g., Josh 21:45; 2 Sam 19:31). In Ecclesiastes it refers to "every aspect of life" (Eccl 1:2; 12:8); in the rest of the book (which contains nearly one-third of its biblical occurrences), it refers to "every example of what I am considering (i.e., in this statement)," whether every human or divine deed (1:14; 2:11; 3:1, 11), all people (2:16), all living things that breathe (3:19–20), and so on.

And so what does Ecclesiastes 1:2 say? Perhaps something like this: " 'A mere breath,' says Qohelet. 'A mere breath — it's all just breath.' "

Since everything "under the sun" is temporary, fleeting, and soon "flies away" (cf. Prov 23:4 – 5), we should enjoy what we have (e.g., resources, time, opportunity, friendship) and what we can do (work, ministry, projects, etc.), and enjoy them *now*, because all of those things will end with us, passing away as surely as we will die. "We should think not of what is 'meaningless', but of what is 'quickly passing,'" says one commentator; "life is a fleeting thing that needs to be savored and enjoyed as a gift from God."[2]

Frederic Clarke Putnam

Notes

1. Cf., e.g., W. Sibley Towner, "Ecclesiastes," in *The New Interpreter's Bible* (Nashville: Abingdon, 1997), 5:290.

2. Earl D. Radmacher et al., eds. *Nelson's New Illustrated Bible Commentary* (Nashville: Nelson, 1999), 781.

A Rhythm of Grief and Hope

LAMENTATIONS 3:22–24

MT	NRSV
חַסְדֵי יְהוָה כִּי לֹא־תָמְנוּ	²² The steadfast love of the LORD never ceases,
כִּי לֹא־כָלוּ רַחֲמָיו	his mercies never come to an end;
חֲדָשִׁים לַבְּקָרִים	²³ they are new every morning;
רַבָּה אֱמוּנָתֶךָ	great is your faithfulness.
חֶלְקִי יְהוָה אָמְרָה נַפְשִׁי	²⁴ "The LORD is my portion," says my soul,
עַל־כֵּן אוֹחִיל לוֹ	"therefore I will hope in him."

As I write this devotion, I am only weeks removed from the events of June 5, 2014. On that day a gunman stepped onto the campus of the university where I teach and began a shooting spree that left one student dead and two students injured. Were it not for the actions of a brave student who disarmed him, the death toll would have been much higher since the assailant intended to replicate the 1999 Columbine shooting. The hours, days, and weeks following the tragedy were filled with contradictions. On several occasions I was overcome with grief. Yet paradoxically, I experienced comfort, gratefulness, and even healing from the very community that had been so badly wounded. This event was our greatest nightmare, yet it also produced our finest hour.

In such moments people are often at a loss for words. Thankfully, we had Lamentations as a resource, and in the various prayer services that followed the tragedy we repeatedly turned to this book. Lamentations is well-known for its poetic devices. One of its more notable poetic features is the acrostic structure of chs. 1–4. Chapters 1 and 2 comprise twenty-two verses or stanzas of three lines each, where each verse begins with a subsequent letter of the Hebrew alphabet. Chapter 4 comprises twenty-two verses of two lines, with each verse beginning with an acrostic letter. Chapter 3, situated in the middle of the book, however, contains sixty-six verses. In Hebrew, these verses are actually twenty-two three-line stanzas where *each line* of each stanza begins with the same acrostic letter. The visual and aural effects of this poetic pattern are stunning and hypnotic, yet sadly acrostics are rarely replicated in translations. English translations generally indicate the poetic pattern of Psalm 119, the most well-known acrostic in the Bible, but they rarely identify such patterns in Lamentations. Even readers lacking knowledge of Hebrew can observe that vv. 22, 23, and 24 of ch. 3 in our devotional passage each begin with the letter ה, the eighth letter in the Hebrew alphabet. Verses 18–20 each begin with the letter ז, the seventh letter in the alphabet, and the verses that follow (vv. 25–27) each begin with ט, the ninth letter. This pattern continues throughout the whole chapter.

This artistry unifies the book and creates a consistent rhythm. Acrostics provide cohesion to poems such that individual verses are never meant to be read in isolation. The temptation for readers of Lamentations is to choose only those verses that appeal to them, whether they are its affirmations of trust and hope in 3:22–36 or the bitter laments that dominate most of the work. Yet just as everyone knows not to begin or end with the letter "P" in the "ABC Song," so too readers of Lamentations know that they are to read each chapter, as well as the book, in its entirety. They are to hear and voice words of *both* distress and trust.

Scholars have been baffled about how to account for these disparate texts within the same book. The experiences of the last several weeks have confirmed to me that these seemingly contradictory texts can stand alongside each other without explanation. For both grief and hope comprise the rhythm of faith and worship. As a colleague of mine shared, "In consolation, remember desolation. In desolation, remember consolation." Such is the rhythm of Lamentations.

Bo H. Lim

A Purposeful Life

MT	NIV
וּמִי יוֹדֵעַ אִם־לְעֵת כָּזֹאת הִגַּעַתְּ לַמַּלְכוּת׃	And who knows but that you have come to your royal position for such a time as this?

With simple Hebrew vocabulary and syntax, this question Mordecai poses to Esther echoes profound insight into life's circumstances. Esther had been taken into the Persian harem and forced to play the new-queen beauty contest, and she successfully won the favor of the ruthless and lustful king Xerxes (2:17). The mystery of a combination of circumstances beyond her control and her own comportment had brought her to a moment of decision, a moment that will forever change her life and the lives of untold others.

At this defining moment Esther is confronted by this question about her purpose in life. Was there any meaning to what had happened to her? What would her life count for? Despite the morally ambiguous path that brought her to this royal position, Esther is invited to reflect on the possibility that God has been working providentially to fulfill his covenant promises and preserve his people for redemptive purposes far beyond the circumstances of the moment. Much is beyond Esther's control, but it all comes down to a decision that is hers and hers alone: Will she identify with God's covenant people or keep her identity a secret and continue to live like a pagan in the Persian court? The lots had been cast to select the day and month for Haman's decree to annihilate the Jewish people throughout the empire (3:7), but what will be Esther's lot in life?

The Hebrew verb נגע in the *qal* stem means "to touch," but in the *hiphil* (as found here, הִגַּעַתְּ) it means "to arrive" in time (not at a location), invoking the image of the passage of time that led up to this moment (cf. Esth 2:2; 9:26; Dan 12:12; Eccl 8:14). Esther arrived at this decisive moment through the will of others, but after her decision, she herself becomes a powerful agent. Her turning point comes when she decides to throw her lot in with God's people, to make their destiny her destiny. And because the roll of dice (*pûrîm* in Hebrew) will never determine the lot of God's people, Esther's life takes on new meaning.

We can relate to that morally ambiguous path that has brought each of us to this moment of our lives today. The most essential defining moment arrives when we identify with God's people through faith in Jesus Christ. Despite circumstances and our own behavior, God works providentially to bring us to that moment of decision for Christ. Each of us then becomes part of a story that is much greater than our own lives, a story of God's redemptive purposes being worked out in human history. Even circumstances that look to be by chance are caught up in God's ways far beyond our knowing (Isa 55:8–9). Our lives take on new meaning and purpose. Esther did not know the end of her story when she was in the middle of it, nor do we. We know only that the thread of our lives is woven into the great tapestry of human history. Much is beyond our control, but through each day we find defining moments of opportunity to live for the Lord through obedience to his Word.

One's life may not be perfect, but it can be purposeful. Esther wasn't in the perfect place. She wasn't a perfect person. She wasn't in perfect circumstances. She wasn't in control of what shaped her life. Yet God worked mightily through her decision to be one of his people. God filled Esther's life with meaning and purpose far beyond anything she could have planned. And so he fills the lives of each of us who have come "into the kingdom for such a time as this."

Karen H. Jobes

MENE, MENE, TEKEL, PARSIN?

DANIEL 1:5

MT	NIV
וַיְמַן לָהֶם הַמֶּלֶךְ דְּבַר־יוֹם בְּיוֹמוֹ	The king assigned them a daily amount
מִפַּת־בַּג הַמֶּלֶךְ וּמִיֵּין מִשְׁתָּיו	of food and wine from the king's table.
וּלְגַדְּלָם שָׁנִים שָׁלוֹשׁ	They were to be trained for three years,
וּמִקְצָתָם יַעַמְדוּ לִפְנֵי הַמֶּלֶךְ׃	and after that they were to enter the king's service.

One of the benefits of studying biblical Hebrew is that the student or pastor can see the underlying Hebrew words that are masked in English translation. Oftentimes, these Hebrew words are repeated in a narrative to alert the reader to key ideas in the stories that are told.

Sometimes, these Hebrew words are so common even a first-year Hebrew student would know them. We have just such an example in Daniel 1, where the common Hebrew verb נָתַן appears. נָתַן is usually glossed "to give" and occurs about two thousand times in the Hebrew Bible. Yet English translations mostly mask its appearance in Daniel 1, where it occurs in three important verses. In v. 2, the NIV reads, "And the Lord *delivered* Jehoiakim king of Judah into his [Nebuchadnezzar's] hand, along with some of the articles from the temple of God." In v. 9, the NIV translates, "Now God had *caused* the official to show favor and compassion to Daniel." The ESV brings out this nuance better, "And God *gave* Daniel favor and compassion in the sight of the chief of the eunuchs." The trifecta of this key word is completed in v. 17, "To these four young men God *gave* knowledge and understanding of all kinds of literature and learning." God is sovereign in the book of Daniel. He is the one who gives and who takes away.

There is another Hebrew word in Daniel 1 that is not as common but is also important: the word מָנָה. It occurs twenty-eight times in the Hebrew Bible and means "to count, appoint." It appears three times in ch. 1: in v. 5, "The king *assigned* them a daily amount of food and wine from the king's table"; in v. 10, "the official told Daniel, 'I am afraid of my lord the king, who has *assigned* your food and drink'"; and finally in v. 11, "Daniel then said to the guard whom the chief official had *appointed* over Daniel, Hananiah, Mishael and Azariah." After Daniel 1, מָנָה no longer appears in the book, but its Aramaic cognate מְנָה occurs in the Aramaic chapters of Daniel (2:4b – 7:28). It occurs three times in 2:24, 49 and 3:12 with basically the same meaning: King Nebuchadnezzar (or his agent) "appoints" or "assigns" and thereby controls events. Its last occurrence in 5:26, however, is different.

Daniel 5 is, of course, the famous "Handwriting on the Wall" episode, where a mysterious hand appears during Belshazzar's feast and writes: MENE, MENE, TEKEL, PARSIN. Here מנא occurs in the context of this word riddle. Scholars have long recognized that the inscription refers on the face of it to units of money: "mina, mina, shekel, and a half." Here "mina" is the Aramaic word מְנֵא, but Daniel connects it by means of a wordplay to מְנָה to interpret it as: "Here is what these words mean: *Mene* [מְנֵא]: God has *numbered* [מְנָה] the days of your reign and brought it to an end." In its final appearance, God is the subject of this verb and it appears in a judgment speech against the king of Babylon.

Thus, מְנָה is a theologically important word in Daniel. The king of Babylon may "assign" food and drink to his Hebrew captives, and he may "appoint" royal officials throughout his realm, but in the end it is the God of Israel who numbers his days.

Milton Eng

Preparing to Teach

EZRA 7:10

MT	ESV
כִּי עֶזְרָא הֵכִין לְבָבוֹ לִדְרוֹשׁ	For Ezra had set his heart to study
אֶת־תּוֹרַת יְהוָה וְלַעֲשֹׂת	the Law of the LORD, and to do it
וּלְלַמֵּד בְּיִשְׂרָאֵל חֹק וּמִשְׁפָּט:	and to teach his statutes and rules in Israel.

How should we prepare to teach Scripture? Although many books, articles, and videos offer step-by-step instructions in the programmatic aspects, Ezra 7:10 illustrates an authoritative and time-tested pattern that will help us prepare to teach Scripture.

In ancient Israel the priest and the king had copies of Torah for personal study (Deut 17:18 – 19). Ezra, both priest and scribe, not only studied and taught Torah, but copied, stored, and preserved the scrolls. Whenever people had questions pertaining to what Torah taught, they went to the priest to inquire. Note Haggai 2:11: "Ask the priests what the law says."

Ezra illustrates an Old Testament pattern of instruction preparation. God sent Ezra on a mission to restore the Jerusalem Judean community, which had been in captivity in Babylon for seventy years. Through the agency of the Persian king Artaxerxes, God the cosmic king commissioned Ezra to help restructure the postexilic community by teaching them the Scriptures. This spiritual reset invites us today.

Ezra took great care in preparing and delivering God's message. The verb and object combination כּוּן + לֵב ("to set the heart [to do something]") may take a complementary infinitive. This tightly structured verse contains three complementary infinitives in parallel structure. The first, לִדְרוֹשׁ, means "to search." When used with Torah it means to pursue instruction. The prefix creates a parallel structure with the next two verbs. The generic word לַעֲשֹׂת, "to do," finds specificity in the context as the elliptical term Torah carries over as the understood object. The third complementary infinitive, לְלַמֵּד, "to teach," with its stated object, "statute and ordinance," completes the verbal sequence.

Ezra followed these three actions in order. He first searched the Torah so that he understood the message. Then Ezra did Torah, which means he lived the message he found in his careful study. He practiced it by applying it to his own life before delivering it to others. Finally, prepared through personal study and committed to the message by applying it to himself, Ezra taught it to God's people. The nominal hendiadys "statute and ordinance" functions like other biblical word pairs (i.e., heaven and earth, land and sea), and probably indicates the totality of the law. The singular suggests a collective meaning "the body of." It is as if Ezra intended to teach it all.

The verbal infinitives circumscribe Ezra's mission in Nehemiah 8. Artaxerxes commissioned Ezra to follow the pattern observed by other priests in the ancient Near East; Ezra must travel as a messenger to a peripheral area, where the national law of Judah's God was not known or understood, and teach it to the people. Ezra fulfilled this task when the people called on him to read Torah, a passage describing the reestablished celebration of the Feast of Booths. Here Ezra fulfills his stated intentions from Ezra 7:10 as he reads Torah publicly (8:1–6), explains it carefully

(8:7–9), and instructs smaller groups of leaders who, in turn, teach others (8:13–15).

Ezra determined to search Torah for answers, live it, and teach it. This prepared him to read it, explain it to the people, and instruct leaders in a smaller group. One can hardly find a more clearly articulated and biblical model of the task Paul addresses in his admonition: "devote yourself to the public reading of Scripture, to preaching and to teaching" (1 Tim 4:13 NIV).

Dave Deuel

God Put It into My Heart

NEHEMIAH 7:5a

MT	NIV
וַיִּתֵּן אֱלֹהַי אֶל־לִבִּי וָאֶקְבְּצָה אֶת־הַחֹרִים וְאֶת־הַסְּגָנִים וְאֶת־הָעָם לְהִתְיַחֵשׂ	So my God put it into my heart to assemble the nobles, the officials and the common people for registration by families.

The value of reflecting on a Hebrew text often lies in paying attention to how its words echo other passages in the Hebrew Bible, both in the book in which the text is found and in the rest of the Bible. When reading Nehemiah, we usually focus attention on his work of rebuilding the wall of Jerusalem, and rightly so (see Neh 1–6). Hebrew vocabulary found in 7:5, however, forces us to consider another dimension of Nehemiah's ministry.

The initial phrases of Nehemiah 7:5a (וַיִּתֵּן אֱלֹהַי אֶל־לִבִּי וָאֶקְבְּצָה) echo words used by Nehemiah earlier in his autobiographical account. The first part is identical to 2:12 where, in describing his night ride, Nehemiah notes what he had not told anyone: מָה אֱלֹהַי נֹתֵן אֶל־לִבִּי ("what my God gave to my heart" to do for Jerusalem). When or how God had told Nehemiah to do this is not explicitly stated earlier in the book, but it likely goes back to his fasting and prayer in ch. 1, when he asks questions about Jerusalem (v. 2), receives a negative report (v. 3), and responds in weeping, mourning, fasting, and praying (v. 4). There, Nehemiah reveals that he was moved by reading the Torah, especially Deuteronomy. This encounter in prayer and Scripture reading is the key to God's placing a mission on his heart, one that according to 2:12 is focused on doing something for Jerusalem.

Clearly the first phase of fulfilling this mission entails rebuilding the wall of Jerusalem, especially since this is highlighted in the report of 1:3 ("the wall of Jerusalem is broken down and its gates have been burned with fire") and is the focus of the night ride in 2:13 ("examining the walls of Jerusalem, which had been broken down, and its gates, which had been destroyed by fire"). But the reappearance of this missional phrase in 7:5 followed by the verb וָאֶקְבְּצָה ("I gathered") reminds the reader that Nehemiah's mission is far bigger than merely reconstructing the wall. The verb used here (קבץ) appears in 1:9 as Nehemiah cites God's promise through Moses to the exiles scattered throughout the nations. God told his people that if they returned to him, he would gather (קבץ) them and bring them home to their land (Deut 30:2–4; cf. 12:5). Thus, when Nehemiah says God put it into his heart to gather the people in Jerusalem in 7:5, this is not an afterthought, but identifies the very purpose of the wall project for which he is so well known.

One can discern in ch. 1 Nehemiah's concern not only for the physical state of Jerusalem, but first of all for "the Jewish remnant that had survived the exile" (v. 2). Motivated by God's promise to his people in Deuteronomy, Nehemiah is broken in prayer and sets out to reconstruct the walls of Jerusalem for the ultimate purpose of gathering the remnant from the exile in the city where God's presence dwells. The following chapters (Neh 7–12) are not mere appendices, but highlight the very purpose of Nehemiah's ministry to his generation: to gather God's people from the nations so they might live and serve in the city of God's presence.

This structure of Nehemiah reminds us to keep our eyes on the priorities of God's kingdom. The provision of physical infrastructure is often important to carrying out the priorities of the kingdom of God, but we must understand this in terms of its ultimate purpose: to gather the community of God from the nations to enjoy fellowship with their Lord.

Mark J. Boda

Is the Position Important?

1 CHRONICLES 29:20b

MT	NRSV
וַיְבָרֲכוּ כָל־הַקָּהָל לַיהוָה אֱלֹהֵי אֲבֹתֵיהֶם	And all the assembly blessed the LORD, the God of their ancestors,
וַיִּקְּדוּ וַיִּשְׁתַּחֲווּ לַיהוָה וְלַמֶּלֶךְ:	and bowed their heads and prostrated themselves before the LORD and the king.

"Show me what position he was in." As I watched in dismay, the translation checker positioned himself on the floor mimicking a dog standing on all four legs. For years we had struggled with translating a variety of terms that refer to kneeling, bowing, and prostrating oneself. In some of our early translation attempts, we had people whose knees were broken (for "kneeling") or people who had tripped and fallen (for "falling on their faces"). There were no culturally equivalent actions among the Apal-speaking people of Papua New Guinea. The closest we could come to the outward form of prostration was a term that could mean kneel, but more naturally refers to squatting. This was not good enough.

English translators have also struggled to capture the meaning of וַיִּקְּדוּ וַיִּשְׁתַּחֲווּ in 1 Chronicles 29:20, as can be seen in this variety of translations: "bowed down to honor" (CEV), "bowed their heads and paid homage" (ESV), "bowed down and stretched out flat on the ground" (NET), "bowed down, prostrating" (NIV), "bowed low and knelt" (NLT). Trying to translate וַיִּשְׁתַּחֲווּ into the Apal language resulted in a phrase that meant "went down completely on the ground and held crocodiles' hands [spread out arms on the ground face down] and was being like he was sleeping dead [lying flat]." I asked one of the Apal translators why they would do this action. He thought for a while before answering, "We might do that when we are sick or when we are trying to go to sleep, but we don't normally do that action."

Numerous ancient artifacts allow us to see the variety of postures used to demonstrate obeisance and supplication in antiquity.[1] Whether asking for a favor from a human (1 Kgs 1:16) or worshiping God (Neh 8:6), the posture was important in antiquity. This is reflected in the various translations of וַיִּקְּדוּ וַיִּשְׁתַּחֲווּ in 1 Chronicles 29:20 cited above. Interestingly, some English translations of 2 Chronicles 29:30 render the second verb in the same phrase with a focus on the purpose of the prostration, i.e., worship: "bowed their heads and worshiped" (NIV), "bowed down in worship" (NLT), and "bowed down and worshiped" (NRSV).

As a translation consultant, I am concerned about both the historical accuracy of the translation and the meaning attributed to those historical actions. For the Apal-speaking people, one possible translation that communicates both the form and the purpose of prostration is a phrase meaning "wanting to lift up God's name [praise God], they squatted down and put their heads to the ground." Another possibility is "wanting to give liver talk [beg for a favor], they squatted down and put their heads to the ground." As the Apal translator considered this second possibility, its meaning struck home. "Oh, you mean he was saying to the other person, 'You are the Big One. I am not.'"

Whether we are standing with bowed heads, kneeling,

bowing down with our heads to the ground, or lying flat on our stomachs like a crocodile, the important thing is that we submit to God and acknowledge, "You are the Big One [Lord]. I am not."

Martha L. Wade

Notes

1. O. Keel, *The Symbolism of the Biblical World: Ancient Near Eastern Iconography and the Book of Psalms* (New York: Seabury, 1978), 308–11.

Hope

2 CHRONICLES 7:14

MT	NIV
וְיִכָּנְעוּ עַמִּי אֲשֶׁר נִקְרָא־שְׁמִי עֲלֵיהֶם וְיִתְפַּלְלוּ וִיבַקְשׁוּ פָנַי וְיָשֻׁבוּ מִדַּרְכֵיהֶם הָרָעִים וַאֲנִי אֶשְׁמַע מִן־הַשָּׁמַיִם וְאֶסְלַח לְחַטָּאתָם וְאֶרְפָּא אֶת־אַרְצָם׃	If my people, who are called by my name, will humble themselves and pray and seek my face and turn from their wicked ways, then I will hear from heaven, and I will forgive their sin and will heal their land.

If you lose all your money, you lose a lot; if you lose all your friends, you lose a lot more; but if you lose hope, you have lost everything. The people living in the impoverished state of Judah during the late-Persian period were in danger of losing hope. The restoration they were experiencing was nothing like the hopes for the kingdom of David as promised by Nathan. The author of Chronicles writes to convince God's people that the promise to David is alive; they should experience the blessing of that promise.

The means to experiencing that blessing is found in God's revelation given to Solomon at Gibeon after Solomon completed all his building projects (2 Chr 7:11); this was twenty years after the previous assembly at Gibeon (1:3). The Chronicler makes no reference to Gibeon on this occasion of the night vision; he has fashioned God's response to correspond to the prayer at the dedication of the new temple.

Hope is a conditional human response. Impact is created through a double protasis. First comes the divine conditional: there will be drought, grasshoppers, and pestilence (2 Chr 7:13). The second conditional is the human responsibility (v. 14a), expressed as a modal sequel with the *waw* translated "if." The promise of hope is the unequivocal apodosis: then I will *hear*, *forgive*, and *heal* (v. 14b). The second conditional is complex but particular: *humble* ourselves, *pray*, *seek* his face, and *turn* from ways of wrong. The author of Chronicles will use each of these carefully chosen terms repeatedly: *humble, pray, seek, turn, hear, forgive, heal.*

A prominent example of this human response to hopelessness occurs during the reign of Hezekiah. In his first month, Hezekiah began to restore the temple (2 Chr 29:3). He extended an invitation to all Israel to come to a Passover at Jerusalem (30:1). This included northern Israel, now ruled by the Assyrians, who had deported all its leading citizens. Many northern citizens responded to this invitation, but they were not ritually ready to observe the Passover. The author of Chronicles uses the formulaic vocabulary in the word of God to Solomon to show how this hopeless situation could be transformed, so "all Israel," not just the citizens of Judah, could be part of Hezekiah's temple restoration and Passover celebration.

The messengers of Hezekiah urged the northerners *to turn* to Yahweh (30:6); many *humbled themselves* and came to Jerusalem (30:11). So many arrived there was insufficient preparation to accommodate them all. Hezekiah *prayed for all the people* as they were resolved *to seek the Lord* (vv. 18 – 19). In spite of the irregularities, *the Lord heard* Hezekiah and *healed* the people (v. 20). The festival had to be extended an extra seven days (v. 23). Hezekiah brought hope to those living in exile under Assyrian rule. They were still a part of the kingdom of David and its blessing. They could experience that blessing in spite of irregularities present in the Passover celebration.

As anticipated in Solomon's great dedication prayer, circumstances are sometimes overwhelming, out of our control. But they must never leave us hopeless. God granted the means of hope in response to Solomon's prayer. God is all we need; but we come to know that when God is all we have.

August H. Konkel

Contributors

John C. Beckman (PhD, Stanford University; PhD, Harvard University) is Assistant Professor of Old Testament at Bethlehem College and Seminary in Minneapolis, MN. He is the author of *Williams' Hebrew Syntax* (3rd ed., Toronto Press, 2007).

Bryan E. Beyer (PhD, Hebrew Union College-Jewish Institute of Religion in Hebraic and Cognate Studies) is Dean of the College of Arts and Sciences at Columbia International University, Columbia, SC. He is the co-author of *Encountering the Old Testament: A Christian Survey* (3rd ed.; Baker, 2015) and co-editor of *Readings from the Ancient Near East: Primary Texts for Old Testament Study* (Baker, 2002).

Daniel I. Block (DPhil, University of Liverpool) is Gunther H. Knoedler Professor of Old Testament at Wheaton College in Wheaton, IL. He is the author of *The Book of Ezekiel* (2 vols.; Eerdmans, 1997, 1998) and *Deuteronomy* (Zondervan, 2012).

Mark J. Boda (PhD, Cambridge University) is Professor of Old Testament, McMaster Divinity College; Professor, Faculty of Theology, McMaster University, Hamilton, Ontario. He is the author of *Praying the Tradition* (De Gruyter, 1999) and *A Severe Mercy* (Eisenbrauns, 2009).

Randall Buth (PhD, University of California, Los Angeles [UCLA]), is the Director of the Biblical Language Center, Israel. He is the author of *Living Koine Greek, Part 1*; *Part 2a*; and *Part 2b* (Biblical Language Center, 2007 – 2008), *Living Biblical Hebrew, Introduction Part 1*; *Introduction Part 2* (BLC, 2006), and *Living Biblical Hebrew, Select Readings with 500 Friends*

(BLC, 2007). He is coeditor of *The Language Environment in First-century Judaea* (Brill, 2014).

Kevin D. Chau (PhD, University of Wisconsin-Madison) is a senior lecturer in the department of Hebrew, University of the Free State (South Africa). His dissertation is entitled, "A Poetics for Metaphor in Biblical Hebrew Poetry."

Robert B. Chisholm, Jr. (ThD, Dallas Theological Seminary) is Chair and Professor of Old Testament Studies at Dallas Theological Seminary, Dallas, Texas. He is the author of seven books, including *A Workbook for Intermediate Hebrew* (Kregel, 2006), *Judges and Ruth* (Kregel, 2013), and *1 & 2 Samuel* (Baker, 2013).

Hélène Dallaire (PhD, Hebrew Union College-Jewish Institute of Religion in Hebraic and Cognate Studies) is Professor of Old Testament and Director of Messianic Judaism Programs at Denver Seminary. She is the author of "Joshua" in the *Expositor's Bible Commentary* (rev. ed.; Zondervan, 2012) and *The Syntax of Volatives in Biblical Hebrew and Amarna Canaanite Prose* (Eisenbrauns, 2014).

Jason S. DeRouchie (PhD, The Southern Baptist Theological Seminary) is Associate Professor of Old Testament and Biblical Theology at Bethlehem College & Seminary in Minneapolis, MN. He is the coauthor with Duane A. Garrett of *A Modern Grammar for Biblical Hebrew* (Broadman & Holman, 2009) and contributing editor of *What the Old Testament Authors Really Cared About: A Survey of Jesus' Bible* (Kregel, 2013).

Dave Deuel (PhD, University of Liverpool) is Academic Dean of The Master's Academy International, a consortium of seventeen seminaries scattered around the world. He is author of "Apprehending Kidnappers by Correspondence at Provincial Arrapha" in *Mesopotamia and the Bible* (Baker, 2002) and "Administrative Mission at Arrapha" in *Tradition and Innovation in the Ancient Near East* (Eisenbrauns, 2015).

Milton Eng (PhD, Drew University) teaches courses in World History and Biblical Studies at William Paterson University and Pillar College. He is also East Coast Project Director for the Institute for the Study of Asian American Christianity (ISAAC) and author of *The Days of Our Years: A Lexical Semantic Study of the Life Cycle in Biblical Israel* (T&T Clark, 2013).

Nancy L. Erickson (PhD, Hebrew Union College-Jewish Institute of Religion in Hebraic and Cognate Studies) is Senior Editor of Biblical Languages, Textbooks, and Reference Tools at Zondervan Academic. She is coeditor of *Windows to the Ancient World of the Hebrew Bible: Essays in Honor of Samuel Greengus* (Eisenbrauns, 2014).

Lee M. Fields (PhD, Hebrew Union College-Jewish Institute of Religion in Judaic Studies in the Greco-Roman Period) is Professor of Bible and Chair of the Department of Biblical Studies at Mid-Atlantic Christian University in Elizabeth City, NC. He is the author of *Hebrew for the Rest of Us* (Zondervan, 2007) and *An Anonymous Dialogue with a Jew* (Brepols, 2012).

Sara Fudge (PhD, Hebrew Union College-Jewish Institute of Religion in Hebraic and Cognate Studies) is Professor of Biblical Studies and Director of Institutional Effectiveness at the Cincinnati Christian University in Cincinnati, OH. She contributed to the "1 & 2 Samuel" commentary in *The Transforming Word* (Abilene Christian University, 2009).

Roy E. Gane (PhD, University of California, Berkeley in Biblical Hebrew Language and Literature) is Professor of Hebrew Bible and Ancient Near Eastern Languages at the Seventh-day Adventist Theological Seminary, Andrews University in Berrien Springs, MI. He is the author of *Cult and Character* (Eisenbrauns, 2005) and *Leviticus, Numbers* in the NIV Application Commentary.

Andrew E. Hill (PhD, University of Michigan) is professor of Old Testament studies at Wheaton College, Wheaton, IL. He is coauthor with John Walton of *A Survey of the Old Testament* (3rd ed.; Zondervan, 2009). He also wrote *Malachi* in the Anchor Bible Commentary (Yale, 1998) and *Haggai, Zechariah, Malachi* for the Tyndale Old Testament Commentary series (IVP, 2012).

Karen H. Jobes (PhD, Westminster Theological Seminary in Biblical Hermeneutics) is the Gerald F. Hawthorne Professor of New Testament Greek and Exegesis, Emerita at Wheaton College in Wheaton, IL. She is the author of many books including *Esther* (Zondervan, 1999). She is coauthor of *Invitation to the Septuagint* (2nd ed.; Baker, 2015). Her commentary *1 – 3 John* (Zondervan, 2014) was awarded the 2015 ECPA Gold Medallion. She also wrote *Letters to the Church: A Survey of Hebrews and the General Epistles* (Zondervan, 2011).

August H. Konkel (PhD, Westminster Theological Seminary) is Professor of Old Testament at McMaster Divinity College in Hamilton, Ontario, Canada. His commentaries include *1 & 2 Kings* in the NIV Application Commentary series (Zondervan, 2006) and "Job" in *Job, Ecclesiastes, Song of Songs* in the Cornerstone Biblical Commentary series (Tyndale House, 2006).

Barbara M. Leung Lai (PhD, The University of Sheffield, UK) is Professor of Old Testament at Tyndale University College & Seminary, Toronto, Ontario, Canada. She is the author of *Through the "I"-Window: The Inner Life of Characters in the Hebrew Bible* (Sheffield Phoenix, 2011).

Bo H. Lim (PhD, Trinity Evangelical Divinity School) is Associate Professor of Old Testament at Seattle Pacific University and Seminary in Seattle, WA. He is the author of *The "Way of the LORD" in the Book of Isaiah* (T&T Clark, 2010) and contributor to the *Dictionary of the Old Testament Prophets* (IVP, 2012).

Tremper Longman III (PhD, Yale University) is the Robert H. Gundry Professor of Biblical Studies at Westmont College in Santa Barbara, CA. He is the author of numerous books including the commentaries *Job* (Baker, 2012) and *Proverbs* (Baker, 2006).

Mark J. Mangano (PhD, Hebrew Union College-Jewish Institute of Religion in Hebraic and Cognate Studies) is Professor of Bible at Lincoln Christian University in Lincoln, IL. He is the author of numerous books, including *The Image of God* (UPA, 2008) and *Power and Grace: A Theology of the Psalms* (Wipf & Stock, 2010).

Benjamin J. Noonan (PhD, Hebrew Union College-Jewish Institute of Religion in Hebraic and Cognate Studies) is Assistant Professor of Old Testament and Hebrew at Columbia International University in Columbia, SC. He has published a number of articles and reviews and is the author of *Foreign Words in the Hebrew Bible* (Eisenbrauns, forthcoming).

Jennifer Noonan (PhD, Hebrew Union College-Jewish Institute of Religion in Hebraic and Cognate Studies) is an online instructor of Biblical Studies for Liberty Baptist Theological Seminary in Lynchburg, VA. She has written "Recent Hebrew Grammars: A Review and Critique" for the *Ashland Theological Journal*.

Frederic Clarke Putnam (PhD, Annenberg Research Institute) is Associate Professor of Biblical Studies in the Templeton Honors College of Eastern University in St. Davids, PA. He is the author of several works including *Hebrew Bible Insert* (Stylus, 1997) and *New Grammar of Biblical Hebrew* (Sheffield Phoenix, 2010).

Brian Schultz (PhD, Bar Ilan University, Ramat Gan, Israel) is Associate Professor of Biblical Studies at Fresno Pacific University, Fresno, CA. He is author of a study concerning the War Scroll from Qumran entitled *Conquering the World* (Brill, 2009).

George M. Schwab (PhD, Westminster Theological Seminary in Hermeneutics) is Professor of Old Testament at Erskine Theological Seminary in Due West, SC. He is the author of a number of books including *Right in their Own Eyes: The Gospel According to Judges* (Presbyterian & Reformed, 2011), "Song of Songs" and "Ruth" in the *Expositor's Bible Commentary* (rev. ed.; Zondervan, 2012), and *Hope in the Midst of a Hostile World: The Gospel According to Daniel* (Presbyterian & Reformed, 2006).

Beth M. Stovell (PhD, McMaster Divinity College in Biblical Studies) is Assistant Professor of Old Testament at Ambrose Seminary of Ambrose University in Calgary, Alberta, Canada. Beth has authored *Mapping Metaphorical Discourse in the Fourth Gospel* (Brill, 2012) and coedited *Biblical Hermeneutics: Five Views* (InterVarsity, 2012) with Dr. Stanley E. Porter.

Chloe Sun (PhD, Fuller Theological Seminary) is Associate Professor of the Old Testament at Logos Evangelical Seminary in El Monte, CA. She is the author of *The Ethics of Violence in the Story of Aqhat* (Gorgias, 2008).

Miles V. Van Pelt (PhD, The Southern Baptist Theological Seminary) is the Alan Belcher Professor of Old Testament and Biblical Languages and Director of the Summer Institute for Biblical Languages at Reformed Theological Seminary in Jackson, MS. He is the coauthor of *Basics of Biblical Hebrew* (2nd ed.; Zondervan, 2007) and the author of *Basics of Biblical Aramaic* (Zondervan, 2011).

†**Verlyn D. Verbrugge** (PhD, University of Notre Dame) was Senior Editor-at-Large for Biblical and Theological Resources at Zondervan in Grand Rapids, MI. He prepared the *New International Dictionary of New Testament Theology: Abridged Edition* (Zondervan, 2003) and He authored *A Not-So-Silent Night: The Unheard Story of Christmas and Why It Matters* (Zondervan, 2009) and *Paul and Money* (Zondervan, 2015).

Peter T. Vogt (PhD, University of Gloucestershire in Old Testament) is Senior Pastor of Trinity Baptist Church, Maplewood, MN. He taught Old Testament at Bethel Seminary in St. Paul, MN for several years. He has written *Interpreting the Pentateuch: An Exegetical Handbook* (Kregel, 2009) as well as other books and articles on Deuteronomy.

Martha L. Wade (PhD, Union Theological Seminary and Presbyterian School of Christian Education in Biblical Studies) is a Translation Consultant with Pioneer Bible Translators in Papua New Guinea. She is the author of *Consistency of Translation Techniques in the Tabernacle Accounts of Exodus in the Old Greek* (Society of Biblical Literature, 2003).

Bruce Waltke (ThD, Dallas Theological Seminary; PhD, Harvard University; fellow at Hebrew Union College, Jerusalem) is Professor Emeritus of Old Testament Studies at Regent College (Vancouver, B.C., Canada) and Distinguished Professor Emeritus of Old Testament at Knox Theological Seminary in Fort Lauderdale, FL. *An Old Testament Theology* (Zondervan, 2007) and *Genesis: A Commentary* (Zondervan, 2001) were awarded gold medallions by the Evangelical Christian Publishing Association (ECPA). He also coauthored *An Introduction to Biblical Hebrew Syntax.*

Brian L. Webster (PhD, Hebrew Union College-Jewish Institute of Religion in Hebraic and Cognate Studies) is Associate Professor of Old Testament Studies at Dallas Theological Seminary in Dallas, TX. He is the author of *The Cambridge Introduction to Biblical Hebrew* (Cambridge, 2009) and *The Essential Bible Companion to the Psalms* (Zondervan, 2010).

Paul D. Wegner (PhD, King's College, University of London) is Professor of Old Testament and Director of the PhD/ThM Program at Golden Gate Baptist Theological Seminary in Mill Valley, CA. He is the author of many books including

The Journey from Texts to Translations (Baker, 1999) and *Using Biblical Hebrew in Your Ministry* (Kregel, 2009).

Michael J. Williams (PhD, University of Pennsylvania) is Professor of Old Testament at Calvin Theological Seminary in Grand Rapids, MI, and a member of the Committee on Bible Translation. He is the author of *How to Read the Bible through the Jesus Lens* (Zondervan, 2012) and *Basics of Ancient Ugaritic* (Zondervan, 2012).

Mark Ziese (PhD, Andrews University, Old Testament) is Professor of Old Testament at Johnson University in Kissimmee, FL. He is the author of *Joshua*, as well as of "Ruth" in *Judges and Ruth*, in *The College Press NIV Commentary* series (College Press, 2008).

Grammatical Terms Index

Brackets [ ] indicate places where the indexed concept is present, though the exact word may not be used.

Hebrew Words Index

185

מָה what, why, 112

מוּת die, 53–54

מָחָה wipe, wipe out, 126

מַלְאָךְ messenger, angel, 42

מנה count, number, reckon, assign, 158–59

מַעֲשֵׂר tenth part, tithe, 89

מַשָּׂא utterance, oracle, 138

מִשְׁפָּט judgment, 80, 123

נְאֻם utterance, 138–139

נְדָבָה freewill offering, 89

נגע touch, reach, strike, 155

נכה [hiphil] smite, 53–54

נַעַר boy, lad, youth, retainer, 59–60

נתן give, put, set, 157, 74–75

סֶלַע crag, cliff, 141, 142

עבר pass over, through, by, pass on, 100, 101

עָוֹן iniquity, guilt, 126

עֲטָרָה crown, wreath, 115

עַם people, 82, 83

עֵמֶק vale, valley, lowland, 51

עשׂה do, make, 161

פסח pass or spring over, 101

פָּרַח bud, sprout, shoot, 30

פֶּרַח bud, sprout, 31

פֶּשַׁע transgression, rebellion, 126

פתה be simple, enticed, deceive, 134–35

פֶּתִי simple, naïve, 135

צְדָקָה righteousness, 123

צִיץ blossom; shine, 31

צֶמַח sprout, growth, branch, 115

קבץ gather, collect, 164

קדד bow down, 166–67

קָטֹן small, insignificant, 59–60

קַיִץ summer, summer fruit, 141

קשׁר bind, conspire, 43

רַחֲמִים compassion, 57, 126

רעה pasture, tend, graze, 79

רַק (adverb) only, 40

שׂכל be prudent, 40

שׁאל ask, inquire, 49

שׁוּב turn back, return, 60

שׁנן [piel] impress, repeat, 34–35

שָׁקֵד almond(-tree), 31

שֵׁשַׁךְ Sheshak, 76–77

תּוֹדָה thanksgiving, 89

תַּחַת underneath, below, instead of, 115

תִּקְוָה cord, hope, 43

Devotions on the Greek New Testament

52 Reflections to Inspire and Instruct

J. Scott Duvall and Verlyn Verbrugge, General Editors

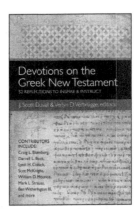

Devotions on the Greek New Testament contains 52 devotions — based on a careful reading and study of the Greek New Testament — written by some of the top Greek scholars of today. Contributors include Scot McKnight, Daniel B. Wallace, Craig L. Blomberg, Mark Strauss, and William D. Mounce, among others.

Devotions on the Greek New Testament can be used as a weekly devotional or as a supplemental resource throughout a semester or sequence of courses. The main point each devotion offers comes from a careful reading of the passage in the Greek New Testament, not from the English Bible. These authors use a variety of exegetical approaches in their devotions: grammatical, lexical, rhetorical, sociohistorical, linguistic, etc. Each devotion closes with a practical application.

Available in stores and online!

ZONDERVAN®
.com

Hebrew for the Rest of Us

Using Hebrew Tools without Mastering Biblical Hebrew

Lee M. Fields

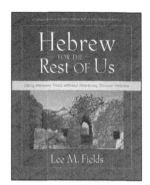

This is a companion volume to *Greek for the Rest of Us* by William D. Mounce. This book is a guide for English-only readers to understand the language of the Old Testament just enough to work with the Old Testament in more detail and to understand the scholarly literature on the Hebrew Bible. Its specific aims are to aid students to learn (1) why translations differ, (2) how to do Hebrew word studies, (3) what the basics of Hebrew exegesis are, and (4) how to read more advanced Old Testament commentaries with greater understanding. *Hebrew for the Rest of Us* is set up in a workbook format.

Available in stores and online!

The Biblical Hebrew Companion for Bible Software Users

Grammatical Terms Explained for Exegesis

Michael Williams

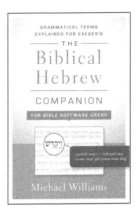

The Biblical Hebrew Companion for Bible Software Users helps readers understand the exegetical significance of Hebrew grammatical terminology identified by Bible software programs, giving them deeper insight into the biblical text.

The Biblical Hebrew Companion for Bible Software Users is ideally suited for:

- Pastors and ministry leaders who may have learned Hebrew at one time but have lost much of what they learned
- College and seminary students who are learning Hebrew and need a guide to help understand the significance of the grammatical terminology
- Bible software users who never formally learned Hebrew in the classroom and need help understanding the meaning of terms they encounter

With grammatical terms laid out and discussed in an intuitive, user-friendly format, readers can now spend time focusing on exegesis and applying their findings to their preaching, teaching, study, and writing, instead of puzzling over the significance of grammatical terminology and how to apply it.

Old Testament Hebrew Vocabulary Cards App

Miles V. Van Pelt

The *Old Testament Hebrew Vocabulary Cards App* is tailor-made to meet the study needs of nearly every biblical Hebrew student.

Features include:

- Over 1,000 of the most common biblical Hebrew words
- Cards linked to 7 popular Hebrew grammars
- Sortable in various ways, including by chapter (in related grammars), by parts of speech, and by frequency
- Viewable alphabetically, by frequency, or randomly
- Test your knowledge with a "Quiz Mode" that tracks your progress
- Pronunciation mode automatically pronounces the word when each new card appears or upon request
- And much more

Go to *zndr.vn/hebrewapp* for more details

Available in stores and online!

Biblical Hebrew: A Compact Guide

Miles Van Pelt

Biblical Hebrew: A Compact Guide offers a one-stop guide for those who have taken first-year Hebrew to refresh their memory on language forms, grammar, and word meanings. Students who are in second-year Hebrew courses can use this reference resource to assist them in the identification of words in the biblical text and the way they are used in sentences.

Ultimately, this inexpensive reference gives the most important information on biblical Hebrew grammar.

Available in stores and online!

Basics of Biblical Hebrew Grammar

Second Edition

Gary D. Pratico and Miles V. Van Pelt

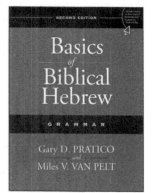

Features of *Basics of Biblical Hebrew Grammar*, Second Edition:

- Combines the best of inductive and deductive approaches
- Uses actual examples from the Hebrew Old Testament rather than "made-up" illustrations
- Emphasizes the structural pattern of the Hebrew language rather than rote memorization, resulting in a simple, enjoyable, and effective learning process
- Colored text highlights particles added to nouns and verbs, allowing easy recognition of new forms
- Chapters Two (Hebrew Vowels), Nine (Pronominal Suffixes), Seventeen (Waw Consecutive), Eighteen (Imperative, Cohortative, and Jussive), and Twenty-Three (Issues of Sentence Syntax) are revised and expanded
- Section of appendices and study aids is clearly marked for fast reference
- Larger font and text size make reading easier
- Updated author website with additional Hebrew language resources and product information (www.basics ofbiblicalhebrew.com)

Numerous student and instructor resources for Basics of Biblical Hebrew Grammar are available on Zondervan's resource website located at www.ZondervanAcademic.com.